New York Mets 2020

A Baseball Companion

Edited by R.J. Anderson, Craig Goldstein and Bret Sayre

Baseball Prospectus

Craig Brown, Steven Goldman and David Pease, Consultant Editors
Robert Au, Harry Pavlidis and Amy Pircher, Statistics Editors

Copyright © 2020 by DIY Baseball, LLC.
All rights reserved

This book or any part thereof may not be reproduced or transmitted in any form or by any means, electronic or mechanical, including photocopying, recording, or by any information storage and retrieval system, without permission in writing from the publisher.

Limit of Liability/Disclaimer of Warranty: While the publisher and the author have used their best efforts in preparing this book, they make no representations or warranties with respect to the accuracy or completeness of the contents of this book and specifically disclaim any implied warranties of merchantability or fitness for a particular purpose. No warranty may be created or extended by sales representatives or written sales materials. The advice and strategies contained herein may not be suitable for your situation. You should consult with a professional where appropriate. Neither the publisher nor the author shall be liable for any loss of profit or any other commercial damages, including but not limited to special, incidental, consequential, or other damages.

Library of Congress Cataloging-in-Publication Data:
paperback
ISBN-13: 978-1-950716-10-4

Project Credits
Cover Design: Michael Byzewski at Aesthetic Apparatus
Interior Design and Production: Jeff Pease, Dave Pease
Layout: Jeff Pease, Dave Pease

Baseball icon courtesy of Uberux, from https://www.shareicon.net/author/uberux

Ballpark diagram courtesy of Lou Spirito/THIRTY81 Project, https://thirty81project.com/

Manufactured in the United States of America
10 9 8 7 6 5 4 3 2 1

Table of Contents

Statistical Introduction v

Part 1: Team Analysis

New York Mets: Where Are You Going, Where Have You Been? 3
    Nick Schaefer, Jarrett Seidler and Matthew Trueblood

Performance Graphs 9

2019 Team Performance 10

2020 Team Projections 11

Team Personnel 12

Citi Field Stats 13

Mets Team Analysis 15

Part 2: Player Analysis

Mets Player Analysis 20

Mets Prospects 101

Part 3: Featured Articles

The Baseball Is Juiced (Again) 117
    Robert Arthur

The Moral Hazard of Playing It Safe 121
    Craig Goldstein

Index of Names 127

Statistical Introduction

Sports are, fundamentally, a blend of athletic endeavor and storytelling. Baseball, like any other sport, tells its stories in so many ways: in the arc of a game from the stands or a season from the box scores, in photos, or even in numbers. At Baseball Prospectus, we understand that statistics don't replace observation or any of baseball's stories, but complement everything else that makes the game so much fun.

What stats help us with is with patterns and precision, variance and value. This book can help you learn things you may not see from watching a game or hundred, whether it's the path of a career over time or the breadth of the entire MLB. We'd also never ask you to choose between our numbers and the experience of viewing a game from the cheap seats or the comfort of your home; our publication combines running the numbers with observations and wisdom from some of the brightest minds we can find. But if you *do* want to learn more about the numbers beyond what's on the backs of player jerseys, let us help explain.

Offense

We've revised our methodology for determining batting value. Long-time readers of the book will notice that we've retired True Average in favor of a new metric: Deserved Runs Created Plus (DRC+). Developed by Jonathan Judge and our stats team, this statistic measures everything a player does at the plate–reaching base, hitting for power, making outs, and moving runners over–and puts it on a scale where 100 equals league-average performance. A DRC+ of 150 is terrific, a DRC+ of 100 is average and a DRC+ of 75 means you better be an excellent defender.

DRC+ also does a better job than any of our previous metrics in taking contextual factors into account. The model adjusts for how the park affects performance, but also for things like the talent of the opposing pitcher, value of different types of batted-ball events, league, temperature and other factors. It's able to describe a player's expected offensive contribution than any other statistic we've found over the years, and also does a better job of predicting future performance as well.

There's a lot more to DRC+'s story, and you can read all about it in greater depth near the end of this book.

The other aspect of run-scoring is baserunning, which we quantify using Baserunning Runs. BRR not only records the value of stolen bases (or getting caught in the act), but also accounts for all the stuff that doesn't show up on the back of a baseball card: a runner's ability to go first to third on a single, or advance on a fly ball.

Defense

Where offensive value is *relatively* easy to identify and understand, defensive value is...not. Over the past dozen years, the sabermetric community has focused mostly on stats based on zone data: a real-live human person records the type of batted ball and estimated landing location, and models are created that give expected outs. From there, you can compare fielders' actual outs to those expected ones. Simple, right?

Unfortunately, zone data has two major issues. First, zone data is recorded by commercial data providers who keep the raw data private unless you pay for it. (All the statistics we build in this book and on our website use public data as inputs.) That hurts our ability to test assumptions or duplicate results. Second, over the years it has become apparent that there's quite a bit of "noise" in zone-based fielding analysis. Sometimes the conclusions drawn from zone data don't hold up to scrutiny, and sometimes the different data provided by different providers don't look anything alike, giving wildly different results. Sometimes the hard-working professional stringers or scorers might unknowingly inflict unconscious bias into the mix: for example good fielders will often be credited with more expected outs despite the data, and ballparks with high press boxes tend to score more line drives than ones with a lower press box.

Enter our Fielding Runs Above Average (FRAA). For most positions, FRAA is built from play-by-play data, which allows us to avoid the subjectivity found in many other fielding metrics. The idea is this: count how many fielding plays are made by a given player and compare that to expected plays for an average fielder at their position (based on pitcher ground ball tendencies and batter handedness). Then we adjust for park and base-out situations.

When it comes to catchers, our methodology is a little different thanks to the laundry list of responsibilities they're tasked with beyond just, well, catching and throwing the ball. By now you've probably heard about "framing" or the art of making umpires more likely to call balls outside the strike zone for strikes. To put this into one tidy number, we incorporate pitch tracking data (for the years it exists) and adjust for important factors like pitcher, umpire, batter and home-field advantage using a mixed-model approach. This grants us a number for how many strikes the catcher is personally adding to (or subtracting from) his pitchers' performance...which we then convert to runs added or lost using linear weights.

Framing is one of the biggest parts of determining catcher value, but we also take into account blocking balls from going past, whether a scorer deems it a passed ball or a wild pitch. We use a similar approach—one that really benefits from the pitch tracking data that tells us what ends up in the dirt and what doesn't. We also include a catcher's ability to prevent stolen bases and how well they field balls in play, and *finally* we come up with our FRAA for catchers.

Pitching

Both pitching and fielding make up the half of baseball that isn't run scoring: run prevention. Separating pitching from fielding is a tough task, and most recent pitching analysis has branched off from Voros McCracken's famous (and controversial) statement, "There is little if any difference among major-league pitchers in their ability to prevent hits on balls hit in the field of play." The research of the analytic community has validated this to some extent, and there are a host of "defense-independent" pitching measures that have been developed to try and extract the effect of the defense behind a hurler from the pitcher's work.

Our solution to this quandary is Deserved Run Average (DRA), our core pitching metric. DRA looks like earned run average (ERA), the tried-and-true pitching stat you've seen on every baseball broadcast or box score from the past century, but it's very different. To start, DRA takes an event-by-event look at what the pitchers does, and adjusts the value of that event based on different environmental factors like park, batter, catcher, umpire, base-out situation, run differential, inning, defense, home field advantage, pitcher role and temperature. That mixed model gives us a pitcher's expected contribution, similar to what we do for our DRC+ model for hitters and FRAA model for catchers. (Oh, and we also consider the pitcher's effect on basestealing and on balls getting past the catcher.)

It's important to note that DRA is set to the scale of runs allowed per nine innings (RA9) instead of ERA, which makes DRA's scale slightly higher than ERA's. The reason for this is because ERA tends to overrate three types of pitchers:

1. Pitchers who play in parks where scorers hand out more errors. Official scorers differ significantly in the frequency at which they assign errors to fielders.
2. Ground-ball pitchers, because a substantial proportion of errors occur on groundballs.
3. Pitchers who aren't very good. Better pitchers often allow fewer unearned runs than bad pitchers, because good pitchers tend to find ways to get out of jams.

Since the last time you picked up an edition of this book, we've also made a few minor changes to DRA to make it better. Recent research into "tunneling"—the act of throwing consecutive pitches that appear similar from a batter's point of view until after the swing decision point–data has given us a new contextual factor to account for in DRA: plate distance. This refers to the distance between successive pitches as they approach the plate, and while it has a smaller effect than factors like velocity or whiff rate, it still can help explain pitcher strikeout rate in our model.

New Pitching Metrics for 2020

We're including a few "new" pitching metrics in the book for the 2020 edition, though unlike last year, these numbers may be a little bit more familiar to those of you who have spent some time investigating baseball statistics.

Fastball Percentage

Our fastball percentage (FB%) statistic measures how frequently a pitcher throws a pitch classified as a "fastball," measured as a percentage of overall pitches thrown. We qualify three types of fastballs:

1. The traditional four-seam fastball;
2. The two-seam fastball or sinker;
3. "Hard cutters," which are pitches that have the movement profile of a cut fastball and are used as the pitcher's primary offering or in place of a more traditional fastball.

For example, a pitcher with a FB% of 67 throws any combination of these three pitches about two-thirds of the time.

Whiff Rate

Everybody loves a swing and a miss, and whiff rate (WHF) measures how frequently pitchers induce a swinging strike. To calculate WHF, we add up all the pitches thrown that ended with a swinging strike, then divide that number by a pitcher's total pitches thrown. Most often, high whiff rates correlate with high strikeout rates (and overall effective pitcher performance).

Called Strike Probability

Called Strike Probability (CSP) is a number that represents the likelihood that all of a pitcher's pitches will be called a strike while controlling for location, pitcher and batter handedness, umpire and count. Here's how it works: on each pitch, our model determines how many times (out of 100) that a similar pitch was called for a strike given those factors mentioned above, and when normalized for each batter's strike zone. Then we average the CSP for all pitches thrown by a pitcher in a season, and that gives us the yearly CSP percentage you see in the stats boxes.

As you might imagine, pitchers with a higher CSP are more likely to work in the zone, where pitchers with a lower CSP are likely locating their pitches outside the normal strike zone, for better or for worse.

Projections

Many of you aren't turning to this book just for a look at what a player has done, but for a look at what a player is going to do: the PECOTA projections. PECOTA, initially developed by Nate Silver (who has moved on to greater fame as a political analyst), consists of three parts:

1. Major-league equivalencies, which use minor-league statistics to project how a player will perform in the major leagues;
2. Baseline forecasts, which use weighted averages and regression to the mean to estimate a player's current true talent level; and
3. Aging curves, which uses the career paths of comparable players to estimate how a player's statistics are likely to change over time.

With all those important things covered, let's take a look at what's in the book this year.

Team Prospectus

Most of this book is composed of team chapters, with one for each of the 30 major-league franchises. On the first page of each chapter, you'll see a box that contains some of the key statistics for each team as well as a very inviting stadium diagram. (You can see an example of this for the Milwaukee Brewers on this very page!)

We start with the team name, their unadjusted 2019 win-loss record, and their divisional ranking. Beneath that are a host of other team statistics. **Pythag** presents an adjusted 2019 winning percentage, calculated by taking runs scored per game (**RS/G**) and runs allowed per game (**RA/G**) for the team, and running them through a version of Bill James' Pythagorean formula that was refined and improved by David Smyth and Brandon Heipp. (The formula is called "Pythagenpat," which is equally fun to type and to say.)

Next up is **DRC+**, described earlier, to indicate the overall hitting ability of the team either above or below league-average. Run prevention on the pitching side is covered by **DRA** (also mentioned earlier) and another metric: Fielding Independent Pitching (**FIP**), which calculates another ERA-like statistic based on strikeouts, walks, and home runs recorded. Defensive Efficiency Rating (**DER**) tells us the percentage of balls in play turned into outs for the team, and is a quick fielding shorthand that rounds out run prevention.

After that, we have several measures related to roster composition, as opposed to on-field performance. **B-Age** and **P-Age** tell us the average age of a team's batters and pitchers, respectively. **Salary** is the combined team payroll for all on-field players, and Doug Pappas' Marginal Dollars per Marginal Win (**M$/MW**) tells us how much money a team spent to earn production above replacement level.

Ending this batch of statistics is the number of disabled list days a team had over the season (**IL Days**) and the amount of salary paid to players on the disabled list (**$ on IL**); this final number is expressed as a percentage of total payroll.

Next to each of these stats, we've listed each team's MLB rank in that category from first to 30th. In this, first always indicates a positive outcome and 30th a negative outcome, except in the case of salary—first is highest.

After the franchise statistics, we share a few items about the team's home ballpark. There's the aforementioned diagram of the park's dimensions (including distances to the outfield wall), a graphic showing the height of the wall from the left-field pole to the right-field pole, and a table showing three-year park factors for the stadium. The park factors are displayed as indexes where 100 is average, 110 means that the park inflates the statistic in question by 10 percent, and 90 means that the park deflates the statistic in question by 10 percent.

On the second page of each team chapter, you'll find three graphs. The first is the **2019 Hit List Ranking**. This shows our Hit List Rank for the team on each day of the 2019 season and is intended to give you a picture of the ups and downs of the team's season. Hit List Rank measures overall team performance and drives the Hit List Power Rankings at the baseballprospectus.com website.

The second graph is **Committed Payroll** and helps you see how the team's payroll has compared to the MLB and divisional average payrolls over time. Payroll figures are current as of January 1, 2020; with so many free agents still unsigned as of this writing, the final 2020 figure will likely be significantly different for many teams. (In the meantime, you can always find the most current data at Baseball Prospectus' Cot's Baseball Contracts page.)

The third graph is **Farm System Ranking** and displays how the Baseball Prospectus prospect team has ranked the organization's farm system since 2007.

After the graphs, we have a **Personnel** section that lists many of the important decision-makers and upper-level field and operations staff members for the franchise, as well as any former Baseball Prospectus staff members who are currently part of the organization. (In very rare circumstances, someone might be on both lists!)

Juan Soto LF
Born: 10/25/98   Age: 21   Bats: L   Throws: L
Height: 6'1"   Weight: 185   Origin: International Free Agent, 2015

YEAR	TEAM	LVL	AGE	PA	R	2B	3B	HR	RBI	BB	K	SB	CS	AVG/OBP/SLG
2017	NAT	RK	18	27	3	1	1	0	4	2	1	0	0	.320/.370/.440
2017	HAG	A	18	96	15	5	0	3	14	10	8	1	2	.360/.427/.523
2018	HAG	A	19	74	12	5	3	5	24	14	13	2	0	.373/.486/.814
2018	POT	A+	19	73	17	3	1	7	18	11	8	0	1	.371/.466/.790
2018	HAR	AA	19	35	4	2	0	2	10	4	7	1	0	.323/.400/.581
2018	WAS	MLB	19	494	77	25	1	22	70	79	99	5	2	.292/.406/.517
2019	WAS	MLB	20	659	110	32	5	34	110	108	132	12	1	.282/.401/.548
2020	WAS	MLB	21	630	92	30	3	35	102	85	123	5	2	.284/.382/.543

Comparables: Ronald Acuña Jr., Mike Trout, Tony Conigliaro

YEAR	TEAM	LVL	AGE	PA	DRC+	VORP	BABIP	BRR	FRAA	WARP
2017	NAT	RK	18	27	135	1.5	.333	0.0	RF(9): -1.1	0.0
2017	HAG	A	18	96	181	8.0	.373	1.0	RF(19): -1.9, LF(2): -0.3	0.9
2018	HAG	A	19	74	222	14.5	.405	0.3	RF(14): 1.1, CF(2): 0.2	1.2
2018	POT	A+	19	73	260	15.4	.340	1.4	RF(14): 1.0, LF(1): 0.0	1.6
2018	HAR	AA	19	35	113	3.6	.364	0.0	LF(4): 0.6, RF(4): -0.5	0.1
2018	WAS	MLB	19	494	125	40.5	.338	-0.5	LF(114): 2.7	3.0
2019	WAS	MLB	20	659	136	49.0	.312	1.4	LF(150): -0.8	4.9
2020	WAS	MLB	21	630	133	43.6	.310	-0.1	LF 3	4.8

Position Players

After all that information and a thoughtful bylined essay covering each team, we present our player comments. These are also bylined, but due to frequent franchise shifts during the offseason, our bylines are more a rough guide than a perfect accounting of who wrote what.

Each player is listed with the major-league team that employed him as of early January 2020. If a player changed teams after that point via free agency, trade, or any other method, you'll be able to find them in the chapter for their previous squad.

As an example, take a look at the player comment for Nationals outfielder Juan Soto: the stat block that accompanies his written comment is at the top of this page. First we cover biographical information (age is as of June 30, 2020) before moving onto the stats themselves. Our statistic columns include standard identifying information like **YEAR**, **TEAM**, **LVL** (level of affiliated play) and **AGE** before getting into the numbers. Next, we provide raw, untranslated numbers like you might find on the back of your dad's baseball cards: **PA** (plate appearances), **R** (runs), **2B** (doubles), **3B** (triples), **HR** (home runs), **RBI** (runs batted in), **BB** (walks), **K** (strikeouts), **SB** (stolen bases) and **CS** (caught stealing).

New York Mets 2020

Next, we have unadjusted "slash" statistics: **AVG** (batting average), **OBP** (on-base percentage) and **SLG** (slugging percentage). Following the slash line is **DRC+** (Deserved Runs Created Plus), which we described earlier as total offensive expected contribution compared to the league average.

One of our oldest active metrics, **VORP** (Value Over Replacement Player), considers offensive production, position and plate appearances. In essence, it is the number of runs contributed beyond what a replacement-level player at the same position would contribute if given the same percentage of team plate appearances. VORP does not consider the quality of a player's defense.

BABIP (batting average on balls in play) tells us how often a ball in play fell for a hit, and can help us identify whether a batter may have been lucky or not...but note that high BABIPs also tend to follow the great hitters of our time, as well as speedy singles hitters who put the ball on the ground.

The next item is **BRR** (Baserunning Runs), which covers all of a player's baserunning accomplishments including (but not limited to) swiped bags and failed attempts. Next is **FRAA** (Fielding Runs Above Average), which also includes the number of games previously played at each position noted in parentheses. Multi-position players have only their two most frequent positions listed here, but their total FRAA number reflects all positions played.

Our last column here is **WARP** (Wins Above Replacement Player). WARP estimates the total value of a player, which means for hitters it takes into account hitting runs above average (calculated using the DRC+ model), BRR and FRAA. Then, it makes an adjustment for positions played and gives the player a credit for plate appearances based upon the difference between "replacement level"—which is derived from the quality of players added to a team's roster after the start of the season–and the league average.

The final line just below the stats box is **PECOTA** data, which is discussed further in a following section.

Catchers

Catchers are a special breed, and thus they have earned their own separate box which displays some of the defensive metrics that we've built just for them. As an example, let's check out J.T. Realmuto.

The **YEAR** and **TEAM** columns match what you'd find in the other stat box. **P. COUNT** indicates the number of pitches thrown while the catcher was behind the plate, including swinging strikes, fouls and balls in play. **FRM RUNS** is the total run value the catcher provided (or cost) his team by influencing the umpire to call strikes where other catchers did not. **BLK RUNS** expresses the total run value above or below average for the catcher's ability to prevent wild pitches and passed balls. **THRW RUNS** is calculated using a similar model as the previous two statistics, and it measures a catcher's ability to throw out basestealers but also to dissuade them from testing his arm in the first place. It takes into account factors like the pitcher (including his delivery and pickoff move) and baserunner (who could be as fast as Billy Hamilton or as slow as Yonder Alonso). **TOT RUNS** is the sum of all of the previous three statistics.

Justin Verlander   RHP
Born: 02/20/83   Age: 37   Bats: R   Throws: R
Height: 6'5"   Weight: 225   Origin: Round 1, 2004 Draft (#2 overall)

YEAR	TEAM	LVL	AGE	W	L	SV	G	GS	IP	H	HR	BB/9	K/9	K	GB%	BABIP
2017	DET	MLB	34	10	8	0	28	28	172	153	23	3.5	9.2	176	34%	.283
2017	HOU	MLB	34	5	0	0	5	5	34	17	4	1.3	11.4	43	32%	.194
2018	HOU	MLB	35	16	9	0	34	34	214	156	28	1.6	12.2	290	31%	.272
2019	HOU	MLB	36	21	6	0	34	34	223	137	36	1.7	12.1	300	36%	.219
2020	HOU	MLB	37	15	6	0	29	29	184	138	28	2.3	12.1	248	35%	.274

Comparables: Zack Greinke, A.J. Burnett, Aníbal Sánchez

YEAR	TEAM	LVL	AGE	WHIP	ERA	DRA	WARP	MPH	FB%	WHF	CSP
2017	DET	MLB	34	1.28	3.82	4.03	3.0	97.7	58	11	47.8
2017	HOU	MLB	34	0.65	1.06	3.08	0.9	97.5	59.6	15.1	49.9
2018	HOU	MLB	35	0.90	2.52	2.33	7.3	97.5	61.2	16.2	51.6
2019	HOU	MLB	36	0.80	2.58	2.51	7.9	96.8	49.9	17.5	48.3
2020	HOU	MLB	37	1.01	2.75	2.95	5.3	95.8	54.6	15.1	48.2

Pitchers

Let's give our pitchers a turn, using 2019 AL Cy Young winner Justin Verlander as our example. Take a look at his stat block: the first line and the **YEAR**, **TEAM**, **LVL** and **AGE** columns are the same as in the position player example earlier.

Here too, we have a series of columns that display raw, unadjusted statistics compiled by the pitcher over the course of a season: **W** (wins), **L** (losses), **SV** (saves), **G** (games pitched), **GS** (games started), **IP** (innings pitched), **H** (hits allowed) and **HR** (home runs allowed). Next we have two statistics that are rates: **BB/9** (walks per nine innings) and **K/9** (strikeouts per nine innings), before returning to the unadjusted **K** (strikeouts).

Next up is **GB%** (ground ball percentage), which is the percentage of all batted balls that were hit on the ground, including both outs and hits. Remember, this is based on observational data and subject to human error, so please approach this with a healthy dose of skepticism.

BABIP (batting average on balls in play) is calculated using the same methodology as it is for position players, but it often tells us more about a pitcher than it does a hitter. With pitchers, a high BABIP is often due to poor defense or bad luck, and can often be an indicator of potential rebound, and a low BABIP may be cause to expect performance regression. (A typical league-average BABIP is close to .290-.300.)

The metrics **WHIP** (walks plus hits per inning pitched) and **ERA** (earned run average) are old standbys: WHIP measures walks and hits allowed on a per-inning basis, while ERA measures earned runs on a nine-inning basis. Neither of these stats are translated or adjusted.

DRA (Deserved Run Average) was described at length earlier, and measures how many runs the pitcher "deserved" to allow per nine innings. Please note that since we lack all the data points that would make for a "real" DRA for minor-league events, the DRA displayed for minor league partial-seasons is based off of different data. (That data is a modified version of our cFIP metric, which you can find more information about on our website.)

Just like with hitters, **WARP** (Wins Above Replacement Player) is a total value metric that puts pitchers of all stripes on the same scale as position players. We use DRA as the primary input for our calculation of WARP. You might notice that relief pitchers (due to their limited innings) may have a lower WARP than you were expecting or than you might see in other WARP-like metrics. WARP does not take leverage into account, just the actions a pitcher performs and the expected value of those actions…which ends up judging high-leverage relief pitchers differently than you might imagine given their prestige and market value.

MPH gives you the pitcher's 95th percentile velocity for the noted season, in order to give you an idea of what the *peak* fastball velocity a pitcher possesses. Since this comes from our pitch-tracking data, it is not publicly available for minor-league pitchers.

Finally, we display the three new pitching metrics we described earlier. **FB%** (fastball percentage) gives you the percentage of fastballs thrown out of all pitches. **WHF** (whiff rate) tells you the percentage of swinging strikes induced out of all pitches. **CSP** (called strike probability) expresses the likelihood of all pitches thrown to result in a called strike, after controlling for factors like handedness, umpire, pitch type, count and location.

PECOTA

All players have PECOTA projections for 2020, as well as a set of other numbers that describe the performance of comparable players according to PECOTA. All projections for 2020 are for the player at the date we went to press in early January and are projected into the league and park context as indicated by the team abbreviation. (Note that players at very low levels of the minors are too unpredictable to assess using these numbers.) All PECOTA projected statistics represent a player's projected major-league performance.

Below the projections are the player's three highest-scoring comparable players as determined by PECOTA. All comparables represent a snapshot of how the listed player was performing at the same age as the current player, so if a

23-year-old pitcher is compared to Bartolo Colón, he's actually being compared to a 23-year-old Colón, not the version that pitched for the Rangers in 2018, nor to Colón's career as a whole.

A few points about pitcher projections. First, we aren't yet projecting peak velocity, so that column will be blank in the PECOTA lines. Second, projecting DRA is trickier than evaluating past performance, because it is unclear how deserving each pitcher will be of his anticipated outcomes. However, we know that another DRA-related statistic–contextual FIP or cFIP-estimates future run scoring very well. So for PECOTA, the projected DRA figures you see are based on the past cFIPs generated by the pitcher and comparable players over time, along with the other factors described above.

Lineouts

In each chapter's Lineouts section, you'll find abbreviated text comments, as well as all the same information you'd find in our full player comments. The only difference is that we limit the stats boxes in this section to only including the 2019 information for each player.

Managers

After all those wonderful team chapters, we've got statistics for each big-league manager, all of whom are organized by alphabetical order. Here you'll find a block including an extraordinary amount of information collected from each manager's entire career. For more information on the acronyms and what they mean, please visit the Glossary at www.baseballprospectus.com.

There is one important metric that we'd like to call attention to, and you'll find it next to each manager's name: **wRM+** (weighted reliever management plus). Developed by Rob Arthur and Rian Watt, wRM+ investigates how good a manager is at using their best relievers during the moments of highest leverage, using both our proprietary DRA metric as well as Leverage Index. wRM+ is scaled to a league average of 100, and a wRM+ of 105 indicates that relievers were used approximately five percent "better" than average. On the other hand, a wRM+ of 95 would tell us the team used its relievers five percent "worse" than the average team.

While wRM+ does not have an extremely strong correlation with a manager, it is statistically significant; this means that a manager is not *entirely* responsible for a team's wRM+, but does have some effect on that number.

PECOTA Leaderboards

If you're familiar with PECOTA, then you'll have noticed that the projection system often appears bullish on players coming off a bad year and bearish on players coming off a good year. (This is because the system weights several previous seasons, not just the most recent one.) In addition, we publish the 50th percentile projections for each player–which is smack in the middle of the range of projected production—which tends to mean PECOTA stat lines don't often have extreme results like 40 home runs or 250 strikeouts in a given season. In essence, PECOTA doesn't project very many extreme seasons.

At the end of the book, we've ranked the top players at each position based on their PECOTA projections. This might help you visualize just how a given player's projection compares to that of their peers, so that even if a dramatic stat line isn't projected, you can still imagine how they stack up against the rest of the league.

Part 1: Team Analysis

New York Mets: Where Are You Going, Where Have You Been?

Nick Schaefer, Jarrett Seidler and Matthew Trueblood

2019: What Went Right
For all of the team's struggles in the first half, the Mets won 86 games and finished closer to the wild card than more touted teams like the Cubs and Phillies. They did so by rallying furiously through the middle of the season to at least be relevant into September.

This was a team that had finished below .500 in both 2017 and 2018, so this was an unexpected thrust at competence. And, even better, a lot of the reasons why the Mets had a winning season are sustainable. Pete Alonso was clearly the best man for the first-base job and, to the Mets' credit, they gave it to him on Opening Day instead of trying to claw back an expensive age-33 season with service-time games. He rewarded them with a 141 DRC+, won the Home Run Derby, finished with 53 home runs to break Aaron Judge's 2017 record of 52, and won the NL Rookie of the Year Award. Alonso paired this stellar on-field performance with an enthusiasm that swept Mets fans off the feet, perhaps best represented by his joyful injection of profanity into their classic slogan, "Let's Go Mets."

Alonso wasn't alone; Jeff McNeil built on his excellent 2018 debut by adding power to his already very strong contact-oriented profile with a 129 DRC+ while covering both outfield corners, second, and third base as needed. Also, he adopted an amazing puppy. Michael Conforto also posted a strong season at .257/.363/.494 and somehow found himself as a third-fiddle in a suddenly potent young offensive core.

Jacob deGrom followed his 2.09 DRA in 2018 with a 2.27 DRA in 2019 and picked up his second straight Cy Young Award. The Mets finally gave him a contract extension to ensure their ace remains with the team for the rest of his peak. Home-grown development triumph Seth Lugo continued to deliver high-quality innings out of the bullpen, and Justin Wilson had a strong season once he returned from injury. Miraculously, Zack Wheeler *and* Steven Matz stayed healthy for back-to-back seasons, and although they were more solid than great, Wheeler held on to most of his breakout 2018.

Bonus round: Jose Reyes didn't play for them this year. Marcus Stroman is cool and good and will be under contract for 2020 as well. Amed Rosario finally took a step forward at the plate, although he remains a work in progress. Generally speaking, the Mets were candid about—and their moves reflected—their plan to sacrifice some defense for offense. Moreover, they successfully executed that plan. J.D. Davis may not have a clear defensive home on this roster, but he still posted a strong 122 DRC+. Wilson Ramos was at least an offensive upgrade on the catcher position of years past, and if he wasn't quite as potent offensively as he had been in two of the last three seasons, he was—for him—unusually durable.

2019: What Went Wrong

It was still the Mets. The grim specter of everything that entails casts a shadow over even the bright moments. For instance, when McNeil was exploring adopting the above-referenced amazing puppy at the Mets' own charity event, he said he'd have to check with his wife first—like any sane person would do before bringing a pet home—and now ex-manager Mickey Callaway sidled over and on a hot mic spouted a bunch of hackneyed sexist garbage. Even if there isn't a triumph to sour, the organization will still lurch or stumble into some disaster or other, caused by bad luck, dark magic, gleeful self-destruction, or some blend of the above. To wit, erstwhile franchise savior and incredibly dynamic slugger Yoenis Céspedes mysteriously shattered his ankles into a million pieces while recovering from bilateral heel surgery. When, or if, he will ever play again remains to be seen, but soon the discussion turned to whether or not the Mets could claw back money from his contract as a result. Reader, they did.

Trying to pick the leadoff "2019 Bad Mets Thing" is a frustrating riddle which has no correct answer because we are drowned in valid choices. Callaway and Jason Vargas threatened and tried to fight a reporter because he said, "See you tomorrow," to the manager. Callaway was somehow not fired—not then—although when you have a tactical genius like this you take the good with the bad.

During the 2018-2019 offseason, the Mets traded a global top prospect and a decent pitching prospect for Mariners closer Edwin Díaz and veteran second baseman Robinson Canó (and his big payroll commitment). While it was a defensible Win Now move, the rest of the Mets' offseason was inconsistent with that mentality—most observers believed they were short on pitching in both the rotation and the bullpen. Even with Matz and Wheeler showing uncharacteristic health (meaning Lugo didn't need to bail out the rotation), the skeptics proved correct as the bullpen posted an ERA of 4.99, including a 6.25 mark in the 9th inning.

That last failing is the one that seemed impossible given the acquisition of Díaz. Sure, the middle relief pool was shallow and underwhelming as projected, but the 25-year-old closer was coming off a 1.77 DRA 2018, where he was arguably the best pitcher on a per-inning basis in all of the majors. And, despite a very good 2.95 DRA in 2019, the results were atrocious. He still missed bats at a prolific rate, but when batters didn't whiff the ball was absolutely crushed—he surrendered 14 home runs in just 56 1/3 innings. The bad defense didn't help him either, with his BABIP jumping more than 100 points from the previous season to .387. Perhaps Díaz was pitching through an injury or perhaps he simply couldn't execute his slider as well with the new baseball; Maybe the pitch sequencing and selection were poor, or maybe it was all of the above. Either way, he turned a number of wins into losses. It's not a huge stretch to say that if Díaz repeated his 2018 the Mets would have squeezed into the Wild Card game after all.

The only other big investment in the bullpen also blew up, although this disappointment was more foreseeable. The Mets jumped the free agent market, as they have done in the past, to bring back former Met and domestic abuser Jeurys Familia on a three-year, $30 million deal, which would ultimately be the third-largest contract given to a reliever last year behind Craig Kimbrel and Zack Britton. Familia, whose command and life have dropped over time in conjunction with shoulder problems, served up one meatball after another and was punished accordingly the tune of a 5.87 DRA with a nigh-identical ERA. Other than Wilson and Lugo, the rest of the bullpen did about what you would expect given the names and resources devoted to it and the lack of internal organizational depth.

Although Canó commands a large salary and is clearly on the back-end of a storied career, coming into this year he had still been a quality major leaguer. One of his strengths has been managing his lower body and avoiding the eyewash hustle that has contributed to Canó posting 11-straight seasons with 150+ games played (as opposed to, say, Dustin Pedroia). The Mets somehow didn't get the memo, though, and spent a media cycle excoriating him for not running out a groundball 110 percent and benched him. Almost immediately after returning, he injured his leg busting it down the line on a likely out.

Another classic Mets "Play hurt!" injury snafu claimed Brandon Nimmo as well. He appeared to injured himself, but the Mets declared it a day-to-day issue and allowed him to play through it for several weeks before an MRI revealed the structural damage that put him on the shelf for an extended run. Jed Lowrie, the rare potential high-end depth piece the Mets of yore have traditionally spurned, looked like a good addition. but then another tentacle of the Mets octopus dragged him down into the pit of "miscellaneous leg injuries." Lowrie went from back-to-back 600-plus PA seasons in Oakland to seven hitless plate appearances in Queens.

Then there were all the little extra losses on the margins. Note: this list cannot possibly be exhaustive. i) bringing in Devin Mesoraco on a minor league deal, then refusing to release him when he realized he wouldn't have the opportunity he thought he would, thereby forcing him into retirement; ii) tendering Travis d'Arnaud and then rage-cutting him two weeks into the season after a gaffe-filled game only for him to reemerge as a contributor for the Rays; iii) releasing Adeiny Hechavarría moments before a roster bonus would accrue.

Last, but certainly not least, the Mets did their best to antagonize and waste one of their most talented players. They spent the offseason evidently trying to trade their young ace, Noah Syndergaard. They then drove him crazy with a meandering and physically taxing pre-Opening Day journey through Florida and up to Syracuse. Next, as one pitcher after another around the league broke out by shifting more and more to a heavy high four-seamer/slider approach—something Syndergaard is particularly well-suited for—the Mets insisted on turning him into a pitch-to-contact sinkerballer. Between that and the defensive sacrifices alluded to above, his ERA ballooned well beyond his peripherals. As the icing on the cake, Syndergaard grew tired of throwing to Ramos—a good bat but a very poor receiver behind the plate—and the organization publicly refused to honor his request to work with another catcher. In fact, shortly thereafter they announced they'd give Ramos a day of rest the game after he caught Syndergaard. It might have been best for all concerned if Syndergaard had been traded this winter so as to allow him to make the most of his potential and to bring in some players more consistent with what the Mets were trying to accomplish, whatever that is.
—*Nick Schaefer*

Prospects Outlook

There isn't a lot of help on the immediate horizon here. The Mets traded their closest potential contributor, lefty Anthony Kay, for Stroman. Lefty **David Peterson** is likely to pitch in the majors for a decade, but isn't likely to be a huge difference-maker. Right-hander **Franklyn Kilome** is still rehabbing from 2018 Tommy John surgery. Lefty **Thomas Szapucki's** return from 2017 Tommy John surgery was only a qualified success—his stuff was only most of the way back and he didn't really handle a full starting workload before being scratched from a planned Arizona Fall League assignment. Lefty **Kevin Smith** and righty **Harol Gonzalez** are more potential back-end types.

It doesn't get much rosier on the upper-level position-player side. Shortstop **Andres Gimenez** headed into the season coming off of a reasonably successful finish to 2018 in Double-A and looked like he might be close to contributing. Instead, he had a season-long slog back at Binghamton, looking diminished due to a changed swing. He remains young and talent, but it's hard to pencil him into any sort of immediate contribution until we see him good again.

What the Mets do have is a lot of high upside players who are a few years away from contributing. Shortstop **Ronny Mauricio** debuted in Low-A on his 18th birthday in April and had a successful campaign that hinted at premium upside. Seven-figure 2018 J2 **Francisco Alvarez** skipped all the way to the Appy League as a 17-year-old catcher in his pro debut and thrived there. The history of teenage catching prospects is highly suspect, but he's about as good as you'll come across given that. **Mark Vientos** and 2019 first-rounder **Brett Baty** provide a pair of potential big power bats at third base.

The Mets also pursued an extremely aggressive strategy in the draft, popping overslot prep arms **Josh Wolf** and **Matthew Allan** in the second and third rounds, then punting rounds four through 10 with cheap senior signs to recoup the bonus money. Allan is the real coup there; he was considered one of the better prospects in the entire draft and is already one of the best prospects in the system and a 101 candidate, which is in theory an absurd get for a third-round pick. As with the rest of GM Brodie Van Wagenen's gambles, only time will tell if it pays off. —*Jarrett Seidler*

2020 Outlook

In a confluence of poor decisions and rotten luck that could only happen to the Mets, Carlos Beltrán, the team's wildly popular new manager, had to resign before pitchers and catchers reported to spring training as a knock-on effect of the Astros sign-stealing scheme in which he played such a prominent role. The hasty, awkward search for a replacement that followed was, if the New York tabloids are to be believed, impinged upon by the looming presence of new Mets co-owner Steve Cohen, even though his role within the team wasn't supposed to become more than financial for another half-decade.

Ultimately, however, the team might have landed in a pot of gold. Luis Rojas is a young, bilingual descendant of baseball royalty (Felipe Alou's son), and he'd been a rising star in the coaching ranks for years before getting this gig almost by accident. He'll oversee a team that confined itself to moves on the margins, a year after Brodie Van Wagenen came in with such swagger and got a bit out over his skis. Dellin Betances and Brad Brach signed one-year deals to deepen an enigmatic bullpen, which now has massive boom-or-bust energy. Rick Porcello and Michael Wacha each signed "prove-it" deals that muddy the waters of the rotation pool, but each has been an above-average big-league starter within the last few seasons, and it's not as though Matz or Stroman have impeccable records of health or consistency.

The only certain addition the team made to its peculiar, high-variance positional mix was Jake Marisnick, who offers better defense in center field than the team has enjoyed since Juan Lagares was young and healthy. Unfortunately, he hits like post-prime Lagares too. They'll pray for returns to health for Céspedes and Lowrie, but those hopes seem remote. By and large, this is a team that

New York Mets 2020

believes its identity better matches a hot finish than a sluggish first half, and their 2020 will be defined primarily by whether or not they're right. —*Matthew Trueblood*

Performance Graphs

2019 Hit List Ranking

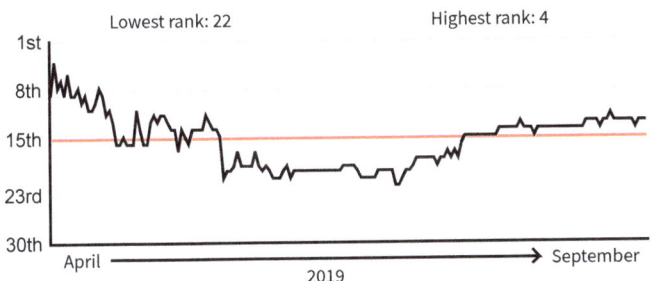

Committed Payroll (in millions)

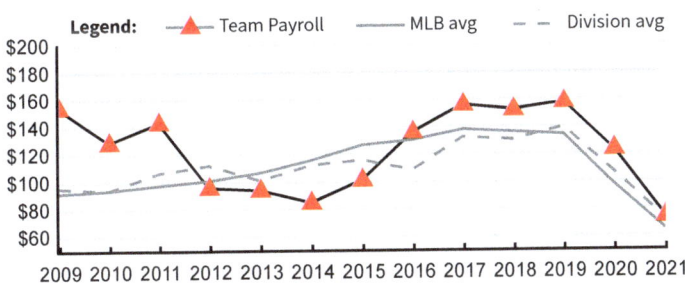

Farm System Ranking

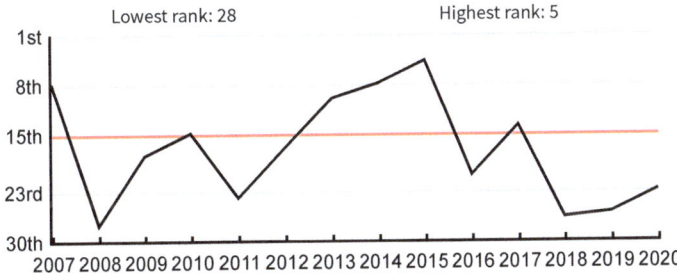

2019 Team Performance

ACTUAL STANDINGS

Team	W	L	Pct
ATL	97	65	0.599
WAS	93	69	0.574
NYN	**86**	**76**	**0.531**
PHI	81	81	0.500
MIA	57	105	0.352

THIRD-ORDER STANDINGS

Team	W	L	Pct
WAS	95	67	0.584
ATL	89	73	0.550
NYN	**88**	**74**	**0.542**
PHI	74	88	0.457
MIA	60	102	0.373

TOP HITTERS

Player	WARP
Pete Alonso	5.3
Michael Conforto	4.1
Todd Frazier	2.7

TOP PITCHERS

Player	WARP
Jacob deGrom	7.8
Noah Syndergaard	5.1
Zack Wheeler	4.2

VITAL STATISTICS

Statistic Name	Value	Rank
Pythagenpat	.534	14th
Runs Scored per Game	4.88	13th
Runs Allowed per Game	4.55	10th
Deserved Runs Created Plus	99	11th
Deserved Run Average	4.11	4th
Fielding Independent Pitching	4.05	4th
Defensive Efficiency Rating	.696	23rd
Batter Age	27.8	12th
Pitcher Age	28.7	21st
Salary	$157.1M	10th
Marginal $ per Marginal Win	$3.8M	16th
Injured List Days	1009	11th
$ on IL	30%	27th

2020 Team Projections

PROJECTED STANDINGS

Team	W	L	Pct	+/-
NYN	**87.8**	**74.2**	**0.542**	**2**
WAS	87.1	74.9	0.538	-6
ATL	82.8	79.2	0.511	-14
PHI	76.8	85.2	0.474	-4
MIA	71.3	90.7	0.440	14

TOP PROJECTED HITTERS

Player	WARP
Pete Alonso	4.5
Michael Conforto	3.6
Brandon Nimmo	2.6

TOP PROJECTED PITCHERS

Player	WARP
Jacob deGrom	6.4
Noah Syndergaard	4.4
Marcus Stroman	1.8

FARM SYSTEM REPORT

Top Prospect	Number of Top 101 Prospects
Ronny Mauricio, #48	3

KEY DEDUCTIONS

Player	WARP
Zack Wheeler	2.4
Todd Frazier	0.8
Juan Lagares	-0.1
Chris Mazza	-0.5

KEY ADDITIONS

Player	WARP
Dellin Betances	1.6
Michael Wacha	0.9
Rick Porcello	0.7
Thomas Szapucki	0.2
Jordan Humphreys	0.2
David Peterson	0.1
Eduardo Núñez	0.0
Ali Sanchez	0.0
Andrés Giménez	0.0
Matt Adams	0.0

Team Personnel

Executive Vice President & General Manager
Brodie Van Wagenen

VP, Assistant General Manager, Scouting & Player Development
Allard Baird

Vice President, International & Amateur Scouting
Tommy Tanous

Assistant General Manager
Adam Guttridge

Senior Director, Baseball Operations
Ian Levin

Manager
Luis Rojas

BP Alumni
Russell Carleton
Josh Turner

Citi Field Stats

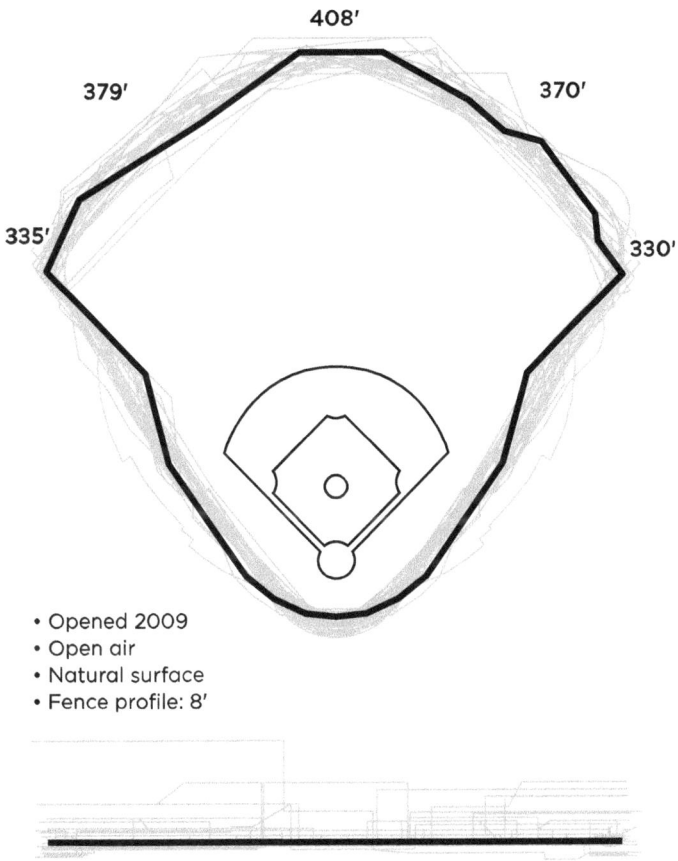

- Opened 2009
- Open air
- Natural surface
- Fence profile: 8′

Three-Year Park Factors

Runs	Runs/RH	Runs/LH	HR/RH	HR/LH
94	93	95	98	95

Mets Team Analysis

Sorry About That: A Letter to My Son

First things first. I suppose I owe you an apology. Before you were even conceived your father and I had decided to split the (then hypothetical) baby—you could be an Eagles, Sixers and Flyers fan, just as long as we taught you to root for the Mets.

It's a difficult row to hoe, made harder by the fact that you're now growing up in the shadow of Citizens Bank Park. And these days the Phillies are trying very hard to be good. It didn't quite work this year, but if they buy all the remaining baseball players, something could really stick!

As a kid, I also spent most of my childhood a Mets fan in Phillies territory. Once, on a field trip to the Vet, the Phanatic gave me a noogie. On. The. Jumbotron. My introvert self has never quite recovered.

And yet. This is a fate I want—I've *bargained*—to pass on to you. Now that you're here, I feel a bit more conflicted. I hate seeing you sad, and should you be as emotionally invested in sports as your father, some tears over a lost baseball game are unavoidable should you follow the Mets. I wish I could promise you it will be worth it, that statistically speaking they have to be good again eventually. But as they well know in Sox and Cubs fiefdoms, it doesn't always play that way in baseball. And this is the Mets we're talking about.

Nevertheless, you deserve a look at some of the finer points of the team. In laying them out for you, I hope the argument for supporting them might yet reveal itself.

But first, a few caveats. A couple things we're definitely *not* rooting for:

- Fraud! Look, being suckered by Bernie Madoff is excusable, or at least it can be—many good people were. But once you start running your own insurance scam, being chummy with Madoff gives off more of a "takes one to know one" vibe. I'm not a conspiracy theorist; it's well known that the Wilpons keep the insurance payouts for injured players rather than invest that money back into the team. Did I mention that one of the Mets' more productive hitters missed the entire season because he fell in a hole? It's curious to me that the league doesn't enforce some sort of protocol or ethical code that would require a change of ownership, unless they, too, have something worth hiding. Alright, maybe I've got a touch of conspiracy theorist in me. Anyway, suffice it to say we're rooting for the players, not the Wilpons. With any luck, they'll be gone before you're conscious.

- Misogyny! It's hard to know why domestic violence is so prevalent amongst athletes. Could it be that those whose egos and livelihoods are reliant upon their physical prowess then turn erroneously to that strength in times of turmoil? Or are they, with lives lived in the public eye, simply getting caught more? Either way, I'd love to simply steer your gaze away from the Jose Reyeses of the world and back to the David Wrights and the Jacob deGroms, but as MLB may finally kind of, sort of, be realizing, ignoring the problem is not going to work. Your dad and I talk often about how to teach you to be a kind person—to be a feminist, attuned to your emotions, to get and give consent. From my perspective, part of that is offering up good role models. I hope as you grow there will be fewer and fewer moments where I'm forced to decide between a love of the sport and love for my son, because that will always mean turning the game off.

- Sloth! The Mets are always finding new and interesting ways to be bad, and this past year was no exception. Credit is largely due to the hiring of Brodie Van Wagenen, who your uncle (also torturing your cousins into Mets fandom, by the way) has very accurately dubbed "the Anthony Scaramucci of baseball." Besides Van Wagenen having only an ancillary knowledge of the sport, it came out midseason that he also couldn't be bothered to actually attend the games, and was attempting to manage from the comfort of his La-Z-Boy. You can't make this stuff up. But you shouldn't root for it, either.

So what exactly are we waving our foam fingers for? Well the talent, for one. Despite the Wilpons' best efforts, we managed to land the most powerful slugger in the league. The rookie Pete Alonso smashed Mets and major-league records alike, hitting a league-wide 2019 high of 53 home runs, and simultaneously breaking Aaron Judge's record for most home runs in a rookie season (52). Alonso won the Home Run Derby and was Rookie of the Year. If the Mets' signature yips don't overtake him, (and if the Wilpons will pay him), he'll be a powerhouse to enjoy for years to come. Jeff McNeil also had a breakout season, slashing .318/.384/.531 with 25 homers and 75 RBI. And despite some speed bumps, deGrom and Thor remained largely dominant, even when they didn't have help to lock down the W.

But with the Mets, fandom isn't all about the win. (Let's face it: if it were, we fans wouldn't exist.) Fortunately, though, there are other bright spots:

- Sloth! You've come into the world too late to enjoy the sight of pitcher Bartolo Colón taking the mound (though weirdly, not *that* late). Though it looks as if Big Sexy's playing days are (finally) over, his accolades remain—he was, in 2018, the oldest active player and the last man standing to have played in the 90s or for the Montreal Expos, and holds the most wins by a Latino pitcher. And just a few years ago he was pitching for the Mets, sending the league's best and brightest down looking with his 90 MPH "fastball" in the NLCS, and catching comebackers with his gut. While Bartolo's beer belly might be evidence for the argument that baseball requires less athleticism than other sports, I think it's intensely charming, a reminder why baseball is America's pastime, a game for the everyfan. DeGrom, while opposite in body type, shares that down-to-earth aura—he keeps limber in the offseason by playing catch with his dad, and has a penchant for Big Macs and Mountain Dew. *Stars, they're just like us!* It's nice when even our most talented Cy Young winners don't have the ego and showboating you get in some other sports, or, say, up in the Bronx.
- Community! You know, Citi Field had a Shake Shack before it was cool.

    It takes a certain constitution to continue to love a team when that team's one true love is blowing a lead. But the people who stick around are ones you'd want to sit next to at a ball game. They find humor in despair; they are pot committed. Famous fans include Harper Lee, Jerry Seinfeld, Chris Rock, Hank Azaria, Itzhak Perlman, and Leonardo DiCaprio-while-getting-hit-in-the-head-with-a-volleyball, to name a few. Not to mention several generations of your own family. Your great-grandma, a diehard fan from the team's inaugural season, bought a tiny Mets hat before she died. Sure, it was probably an accident of online shopping by a near octogenarian. But I like to think she knew you were coming.
- Hope! This year is gonna be the year, I can feel it. Maybe Steve Cohen really will purchase the team and spend money to pay good players. Maybe the return of Carlos Beltrán to the team, this time as manager, will warm up the Mets bats so that poor deGrom can get a win once and a while. Maybe Alonso will continue to be an absolute stud and get a long, fat contract befitting of his talent and the large market team for which he plays. Maybe Yoenis Céspedes will climb out of that hole. Maybe, this time, they won't blow it.

New York Mets 2020

The Mets are the poster team for being so close. They're not bad like, Orioles bad. They're always nearly good. It can be heartbreaking, these near misses, but it is also exhilarating. Watching the Mets reminds me that there's always a little bit of hope, even if it is against the odds. Maybe especially then. In these dark times, hope is a good thing to practice.

    Do you want to know a secret? If, one day, after being humiliated in front of your friends by a man wearing a green shag carpet, you came to me and said you didn't want to root for the Mets anymore, I wouldn't press the issue. I might even take you out and buy you the gear for some other team (or at least send your dad to do it). But I hope that can I raise you to be the kind of person who *wants* to be a Mets fan, someone with the patience to see the diamond for the coal: that is, an optimist.

—Sara Nović is an author of Baseball Prospectus.

Part 2: Player Analysis

PLAYER COMMENTS WITH GRAPHS

Matt Adams 1B
Born: 08/31/88 Age: 31 Bats: L Throws: R
Height: 6'3" Weight: 245 Origin: Round 23, 2009 Draft (#699 overall)

YEAR	TEAM	LVL	AGE	PA	R	2B	3B	HR	RBI	BB	K	SB	CS	AVG/OBP/SLG
2017	SLN	MLB	28	53	4	2	0	1	7	4	17	0	0	.292/.340/.396
2017	ATL	MLB	28	314	42	20	1	19	58	19	71	0	0	.271/.315/.543
2018	WAS	MLB	29	277	37	9	0	18	48	24	55	0	0	.257/.332/.510
2018	SLN	MLB	29	60	5	1	0	3	9	3	18	0	0	.158/.200/.333
2019	WAS	MLB	30	333	42	14	0	20	56	20	115	0	0	.226/.276/.465
2020	WAS	MLB	31	251	31	10	0	14	38	16	76	1	0	.233/.288/.463

Comparables: C.J. Cron, Mitch Moreland, Michael Cuddyer

At age 30, Adams was the youngest player to regularly play first base for the Nationals in 2019, shouldering the bulk of the season while Ryan Zimmerman recovered from a foot injury. Adams' at-bats played much younger, however, regressing to an astounding 35 percent strikeout rate, almost 10 percentage points higher than his previous career-high. A shoulder injury iced much of his August and September, and he remains who he's projected to be for much of his tenure in the majors: a bench player who can still manage to pop 20 home runs.

YEAR	TEAM	LVL	AGE	PA	DRC+	VORP	BABIP	BRR	FRAA	WARP
2017	SLN	MLB	28	53	106	1.8	.419	-0.1	LF(6): -0.3, 1B(3): 0.1	0.2
2017	ATL	MLB	28	314	109	13.6	.294	-0.6	1B(59): -3.3, LF(13): 0.5	0.6
2018	WAS	MLB	29	277	110	10.8	.261	-2.3	1B(48): 0.3, LF(15): 0.7	0.7
2018	SLN	MLB	29	60	115	-3.1	.167	0.0	1B(15): -0.5	0.2
2019	WAS	MLB	30	333	85	-0.9	.284	-1.7	1B(79): -2.9	-0.5
2020	WAS	MLB	31	251	93	5.0	.281	-0.9	1B 0, LF 0	0.5

Matt Adams, continued

Batted Ball Distribution

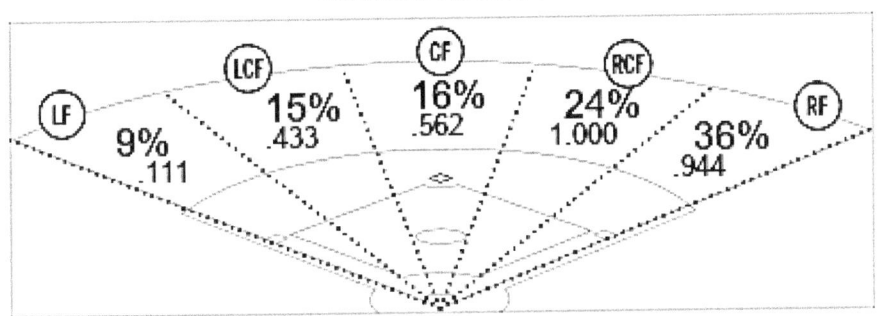

| Strike Zone vs LHP | Strike Zone vs RHP |

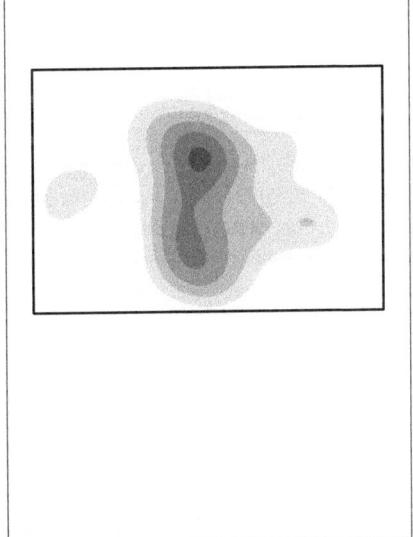

New York Mets 2020

Pete Alonso 1B

Born: 12/07/94 Age: 25 Bats: R Throws: R
Height: 6'3" Weight: 245 Origin: Round 2, 2016 Draft (#64 overall)

YEAR	TEAM	LVL	AGE	PA	R	2B	3B	HR	RBI	BB	K	SB	CS	AVG/OBP/SLG
2017	SLU	A+	22	346	45	23	0	16	58	25	64	3	4	.286/.361/.516
2017	BIN	AA	22	47	7	4	1	2	5	2	7	0	0	.311/.340/.578
2018	BIN	AA	23	273	42	12	0	15	52	43	50	0	2	.314/.440/.573
2018	LVG	AAA	23	301	50	19	1	21	67	33	78	0	1	.260/.355/.585
2019	NYN	MLB	24	693	103	30	2	53	120	72	183	1	0	.260/.358/.583
2020	NYN	MLB	25	630	98	28	1	48	118	63	169	1	1	.256/.349/.570

Comparables: AJ Reed, Ryan O'Hearn, Brandon Allen

For a franchise that seems to be cursed by the baseball gods, they were certainly blessed with a franchise cornerstone whose baseball abilities were equally matched by his off-the-field persona and leadership qualities. That person of course was David Wright but the team was gifted another player who perfectly lives up to that high blue and orange standard and this one is also a bear. From the pomp of starting a jersey-ripping tradition for walk-offs to the custom cleats that he bought his teammates to honor first responders and 9/11 victims, Alonso has attempted to check all of the makeup boxes in just a single endearing season.

The Mets bucked the trend of keeping rookies in the minors to start the season and were rewarded handsomely for their decision. April 12th could have been the date where the slugger made his debut had service time factored into the team's decision-making; between Opening Day and that date Alonso hit .378/.451/.911 with six homers, six doubles, 17 RBI and an eye-popping 1.362 OPS. It was a good move for all involved, except for the folks who have to rewrite the books. If Alonso was in the minors to start the year, he would not have broken the MLB rookie home run record or the franchise records for extra base hits, total bases and hits by a rookie in a single season. This past season was truly a special one both on and off the field for the National League Rookie of the Year and fans everywhere got to witness the birth of a star in the making.

YEAR	TEAM	LVL	AGE	PA	DRC+	VORP	BABIP	BRR	FRAA	WARP
2017	SLU	A+	22	346	168	12.8	.314	-5.8	1B(78): 3.2	2.2
2017	BIN	AA	22	47	104	3.2	.333	-0.1	1B(5): 0.1	0.1
2018	BIN	AA	23	273	180	30.5	.344	-1.6	1B(51): 1.8	2.6
2018	LVG	AAA	23	301	122	14.6	.284	1.2	1B(59): 5.0	1.8
2019	NYN	MLB	24	693	141	47.7	.280	0.5	1B(156): 6.1	5.3
2020	NYN	MLB	25	630	138	43.8	.280	0.2	1B 6	5.1

Pete Alonso, continued

Batted Ball Distribution

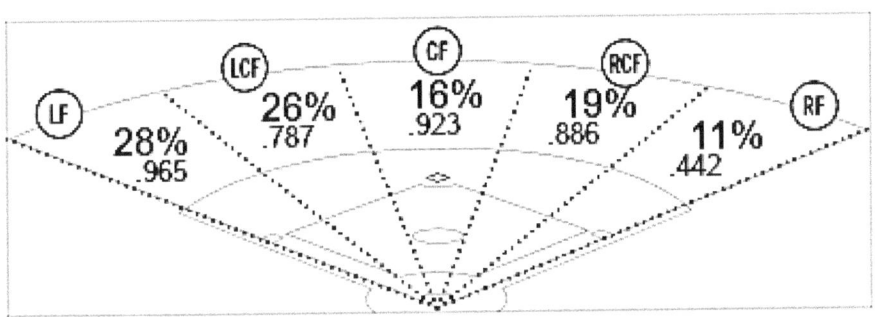

Strike Zone vs LHP   Strike Zone vs RHP

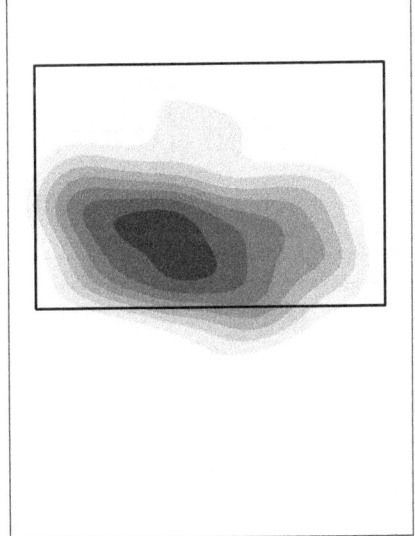

Robinson Canó 2B

Born: 10/22/82 Age: 37 Bats: L Throws: R
Height: 6'0" Weight: 210 Origin: International Free Agent, 2001

YEAR	TEAM	LVL	AGE	PA	R	2B	3B	HR	RBI	BB	K	SB	CS	AVG/OBP/SLG
2017	SEA	MLB	34	648	79	33	0	23	97	49	85	1	0	.280/.338/.453
2018	SEA	MLB	35	348	44	22	0	10	50	32	47	0	0	.303/.374/.471
2019	NYN	MLB	36	423	46	28	0	13	39	25	69	0	0	.256/.307/.428
2020	NYN	MLB	37	525	57	26	0	18	65	35	91	2	1	.256/.312/.426

Comparables: Brandon Phillips, Howie Kendrick, Adam Kennedy

Ask any ruffled Mets fan about Canó and they will probably respond with their best Comic Book Guy three-word diatribe. It wasn't always like this though. Opening Day was a simpler time, in which at least for a brief moment everything went the way it was supposed to. Canó took Max Scherzer deep and Edwin Díaz preserved the lead for Jacob deGrom, giving the Mets a victory to start the season. But happy stories are not the Mets' forte and over the remainder of the first half of the season, Canó had a paltry .628 OPS with eroding plate discipline and little-to-no power. The veteran second baseman came out of the break a new man (well, a rejuvenated one at least) and put up a second-half OPS of .896 until a torn hamstring sidelined him into September. Were he not making nearly $100 million over the next four years of his deal and were Jarred Kelenic not part of the return to get him, Canó might be talked about as an invaluable mentor in the clubhouse to Amed Rosario and gave Pete Alonso sound advice for the Home Run Derby. But if you think it's bad now, wait until you see the discourse in 2022.

YEAR	TEAM	LVL	AGE	PA	DRC+	VORP	BABIP	BRR	FRAA	WARP
2017	SEA	MLB	34	648	108	22.6	.294	-2.0	2B(150): -7.3	1.7
2018	SEA	MLB	35	348	125	23.2	.329	-0.4	2B(69): -2.5, 1B(14): 0.3	1.8
2019	NYN	MLB	36	423	89	7.9	.280	-0.7	2B(99): -7.4	0.0
2020	NYN	MLB	37	525	93	15.5	.281	-1.1	2B -6	1.0

Robinson Canó, continued

Batted Ball Distribution

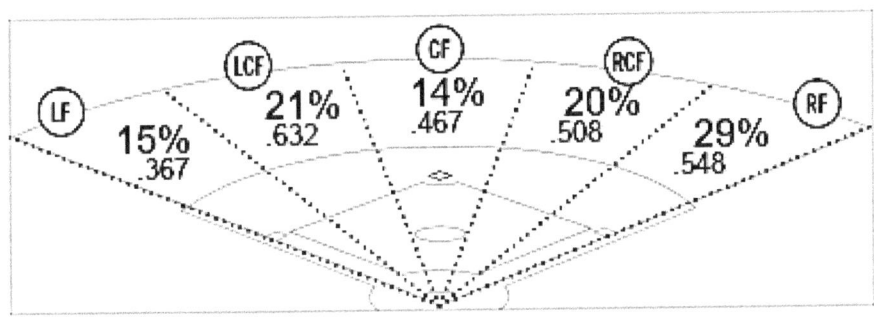

Strike Zone vs LHP   Strike Zone vs RHP

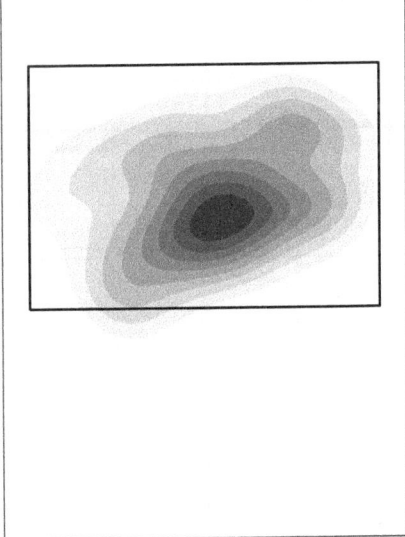

Michael Conforto RF

Born: 03/01/93 Age: 27 Bats: L Throws: R
Height: 6'1" Weight: 215 Origin: Round 1, 2014 Draft (#10 overall)

YEAR	TEAM	LVL	AGE	PA	R	2B	3B	HR	RBI	BB	K	SB	CS	AVG/OBP/SLG
2017	NYN	MLB	24	440	72	20	1	27	68	57	113	2	0	.279/.384/.555
2018	NYN	MLB	25	638	78	25	1	28	82	84	159	3	4	.243/.350/.448
2019	NYN	MLB	26	648	90	29	1	33	92	84	149	7	2	.257/.363/.494
2020	NYN	MLB	27	595	83	24	1	33	93	73	138	3	2	.253/.355/.498

Comparables: Kyle Schwarber, Bryce Harper, Matt Joyce

Conforto quietly had his best season in 2019, putting up career highs in home runs, RBI, hits, doubles and runs. He blasted the 100th home run of his career and his first walk-off was a memorable one when he survived a Polar Bear attack and ended up shirtless in front of a frenzied Citi Field crowd. That signature moment led to many walk-off, shirts-off celebrations from that point on. But the quiet star in Queens also took a different part of his game to a new level without any fanfare: his defense. Already known as someone who could fake it in center when needed, Conforto played his first full season in right field and was a top-five defender by FRAA in that corner. And with two years left until free agency, it's a good time to be showing off his well-roundedness.

YEAR	TEAM	LVL	AGE	PA	DRC+	VORP	BABIP	BRR	FRAA	WARP
2017	NYN	MLB	24	440	133	47.7	.328	1.4	LF(52): 3.9, CF(43): -3.6	3.3
2018	NYN	MLB	25	638	112	36.9	.289	-4.2	LF(84): 1.1, CF(58): -7.3	1.8
2019	NYN	MLB	26	648	122	36.4	.290	-0.3	RF(132): 10.0, CF(39): -3.7	4.1
2020	NYN	MLB	27	595	123	29.9	.282	-0.9	RF 9	4.1

Michael Conforto, continued

Batted Ball Distribution

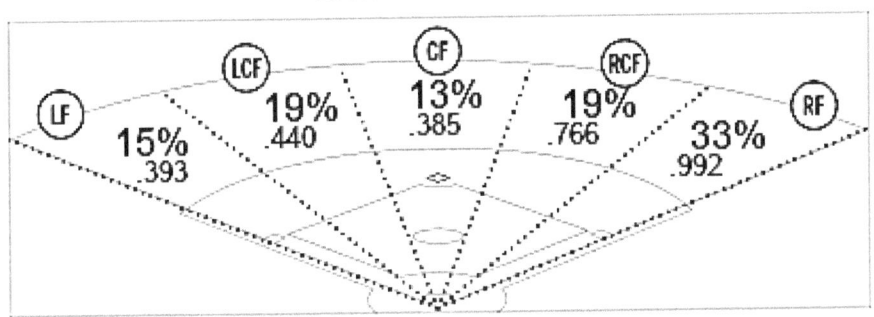

Strike Zone vs LHP   Strike Zone vs RHP

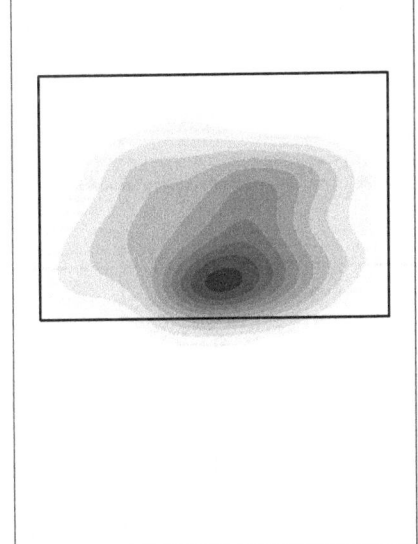

Ryan Cordell OF

Born: 03/31/92 Age: 28 Bats: R Throws: R
Height: 6'4" Weight: 195 Origin: Round 11, 2013 Draft (#340 overall)

YEAR	TEAM	LVL	AGE	PA	R	2B	3B	HR	RBI	BB	K	SB	CS	AVG/OBP/SLG
2017	CSP	AAA	25	292	49	18	5	10	45	25	65	9	4	.284/.349/.506
2018	CHR	AAA	26	193	15	9	2	3	22	11	44	7	2	.239/.281/.364
2018	CHA	MLB	26	40	3	1	0	1	4	0	15	0	0	.108/.125/.216
2019	CHR	AAA	27	55	8	5	1	1	6	4	17	1	1	.275/.327/.471
2019	CHA	MLB	27	247	22	8	0	7	24	19	69	3	1	.221/.290/.355
2020	CHA	MLB	28	251	26	10	1	9	30	16	72	5	2	.220/.278/.390

Comparables: Matthew den Dekker, Scott Cousins, Johnny Field

"That's a goshdang ballplayer," several scouts have surely exclaimed while laying eyes upon Cordell, an idyllically long and lean, athletic and fleet-footed outfielder. Blessed with plus speed and raw power, everything looks perfect when he's gliding at full-tilt toward a sinking flare, or when he squares up a fastball. Unfortunately, he doesn't do the latter often enough. Cordell spins off the ball in his swing and is slow to make adjustments to how he's attacked at the plate. Those would be acceptable sins six years ago given his innate physical characteristics. These days? He'll turn 28 right after Opening Day 2020, and it's time for him to become a fourth outfielder or not.

YEAR	TEAM	LVL	AGE	PA	DRC+	VORP	BABIP	BRR	FRAA	WARP
2017	CSP	AAA	25	292	100	12.4	.339	1.6	RF(29): 0.0, LF(15): 0.2	0.9
2018	CHR	AAA	26	193	79	-0.1	.293	0.4	CF(22): -0.2, RF(13): -0.4	0.5
2018	CHA	MLB	26	40	61	-3.4	.130	0.4	RF(9): -0.3, CF(7): -0.6	-0.1
2019	CHR	AAA	27	55	74	-3.3	.394	-2.9	RF(8): 0.5, CF(3): -0.1	-0.3
2019	CHA	MLB	27	247	68	-3.6	.287	-0.5	RF(72): 1.5, CF(19): 2.6	0.0
2020	CHA	MLB	28	251	74	-0.6	.279	-0.1	RF 1, CF 1	0.2

Ryan Cordell, continued

Batted Ball Distribution

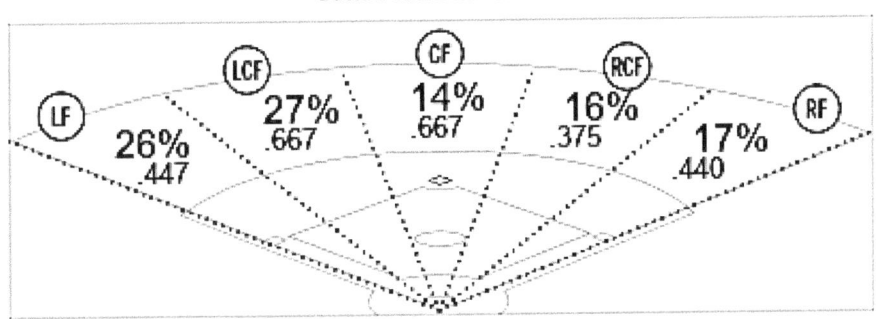

Strike Zone vs LHP   Strike Zone vs RHP

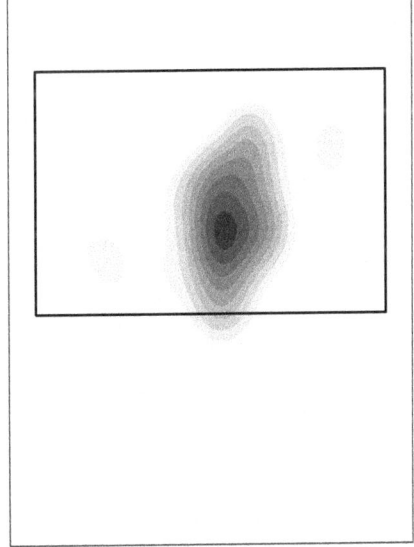

J.D. Davis LF

Born: 04/27/93   Age: 27   Bats: R   Throws: R
Height: 6'3"   Weight: 225   Origin: Round 3, 2014 Draft (#75 overall)

YEAR	TEAM	LVL	AGE	PA	R	2B	3B	HR	RBI	BB	K	SB	CS	AVG/OBP/SLG
2017	CCH	AA	24	388	49	18	0	21	60	31	90	5	2	.279/.340/.510
2017	FRE	AAA	24	73	10	5	0	5	18	9	18	0	0	.295/.370/.623
2017	HOU	MLB	24	68	8	4	0	4	7	4	20	1	1	.226/.279/.484
2018	FRE	AAA	25	377	56	25	2	17	81	36	69	3	0	.342/.406/.583
2018	HOU	MLB	25	113	9	2	0	1	5	10	29	0	0	.175/.248/.223
2019	NYN	MLB	26	453	65	22	1	22	57	38	97	3	0	.307/.369/.527
2020	NYN	MLB	27	455	58	19	1	23	67	36	108	1	1	.260/.325/.477

Comparables: Eric Hinske, Will Middlebrooks, Josh Fields

The trade that brought Davis to Queens in January of 2019 was met with a resounding "why?" After all, they had just signed Jed Lowrie to shore up the infield, which freed up Jeff McNeil to play on the grass—so spending some of their precious prospect capital on a four-corners type to add to the mix seemed suspect. Of course, if Brodie didn't consult PECOTA on the matter, he can certainly pretend he did as Davis almost exactly hit the 122 DRC+ he was projected for heading into the 2019 season. The presumption in Murphy's Law didn't hurt either, as Davis turned quickly from a depth move to, plot twist, an actual offensive threat playing regularly for the Mets. In the second half of the year, Davis was brilliant at the plate and his .979 OPS made him one of the best offensive outfielders in the league. Defensively, he was not so brilliant, but his goofy celebrations made him must-see TV. Keep a camera on that man at all times.

YEAR	TEAM	LVL	AGE	PA	DRC+	VORP	BABIP	BRR	FRAA	WARP
2017	CCH	AA	24	388	137	31.5	.317	-0.5	3B(73): 6.1, 1B(3): -0.2	3.2
2017	FRE	AAA	24	73	138	8.0	.317	-0.4	3B(13): 2.1, 1B(4): 0.0	0.7
2017	HOU	MLB	24	68	78	1.8	.256	-0.2	3B(22): 0.5, 1B(2): 0.0	0.1
2018	FRE	AAA	25	377	158	39.5	.385	0.0	3B(51): 4.2, LF(11): -0.8	4.2
2018	HOU	MLB	25	113	68	-7.4	.233	-0.5	3B(23): 0.9, 1B(13): 0.0	0.0
2019	NYN	MLB	26	453	122	27.0	.355	0.4	LF(79): -4.9, 3B(31): -0.5	2.1
2020	NYN	MLB	27	455	111	18.6	.298	-0.2	LF -6, 3B 2	1.5

J.D. Davis, continued

Batted Ball Distribution

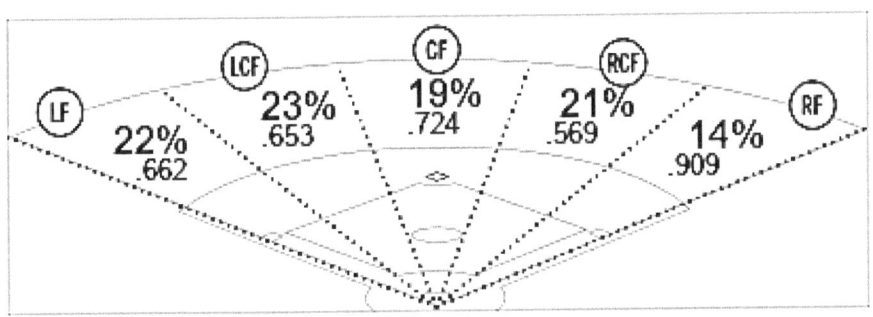

Strike Zone vs LHP

Strike Zone vs RHP

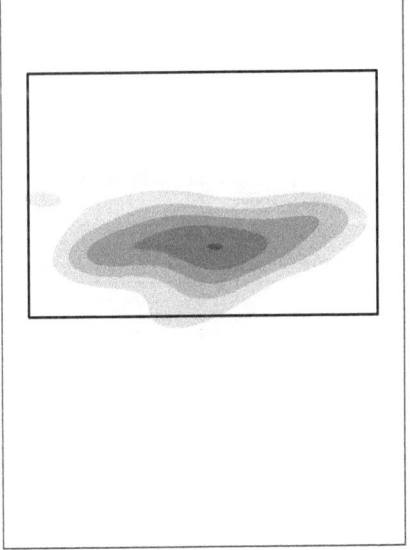

Carlos Gómez CF

Born: 12/04/85 Age: 34 Bats: R Throws: R
Height: 6'3" Weight: 220 Origin: International Free Agent, 2002

YEAR	TEAM	LVL	AGE	PA	R	2B	3B	HR	RBI	BB	K	SB	CS	AVG/OBP/SLG
2017	TEX	MLB	31	426	51	23	1	17	51	31	127	13	5	.255/.340/.462
2018	TBA	MLB	32	408	42	15	2	9	32	25	103	12	3	.208/.298/.336
2019	SYR	AAA	33	140	16	9	1	6	22	8	29	5	5	.270/.329/.500
2019	NYN	MLB	33	99	10	3	0	3	10	7	30	4	1	.198/.278/.337
2020	NYN	MLB	34	251	27	10	1	8	28	17	73	7	3	.216/.292/.376

Comparables: Milton Bradley, Cameron Maybin, Alejandro De Aza

Gómez completed his Mets circle of life when he returned to the team after being traded for Johan Santana in 2008. (He almost made his return earlier in the infamous Wilmer Flores Trade That Wasn't Made in 2015.) Injuries and underperformance opened up the door for him to have a memorable day against the Nationals where he lost a shoe and blasted a game-winning home run, causing fans to lose their minds. As it goes in baseball, the magic didn't last; he was designated for assignment in July, which finally closed the book on this Mets saga. For now.

YEAR	TEAM	LVL	AGE	PA	DRC+	VORP	BABIP	BRR	FRAA	WARP
2017	TEX	MLB	31	426	101	16.8	.336	-0.7	CF(102): -2.3	1.2
2018	TBA	MLB	32	408	84	-0.7	.266	3.6	RF(100): 5.4, CF(4): -0.1	1.0
2019	SYR	AAA	33	140	102	7.0	.301	0.0	CF(23): 1.5, RF(1): -0.1	0.5
2019	NYN	MLB	33	99	73	-0.2	.259	0.5	CF(22): 0.1, LF(13): -0.4	0.1
2020	NYN	MLB	34	251	76	0.7	.279	0.4	CF 0, RF 1	0.2

Carlos Gómez, continued

Batted Ball Distribution

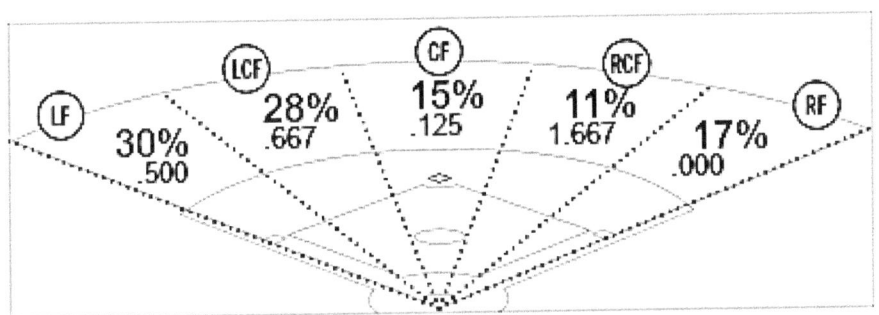

Strike Zone vs LHP Strike Zone vs RHP

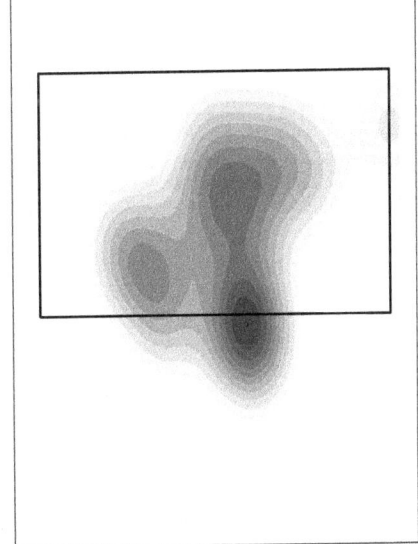

Jake Marisnick CF

Born: 03/30/91 Age: 29 Bats: R Throws: R
Height: 6'4" Weight: 220 Origin: Round 3, 2009 Draft (#104 overall)

YEAR	TEAM	LVL	AGE	PA	R	2B	3B	HR	RBI	BB	K	SB	CS	AVG/OBP/SLG
2017	HOU	MLB	26	259	50	10	0	16	35	20	90	9	4	.243/.319/.496
2018	FRE	AAA	27	82	18	8	2	4	13	6	17	3	1	.342/.402/.671
2018	HOU	MLB	27	235	34	8	1	10	28	15	84	6	2	.211/.275/.399
2019	HOU	MLB	28	318	46	16	3	10	34	17	95	10	3	.233/.289/.411
2020	NYN	MLB	29	322	33	13	1	12	38	18	101	11	4	.208/.266/.380

Comparables: Marcell Ozuna, Gregory Polanco, Jeremy Hermida

Despite starting fewer than half of Houston's games this year, Marisnick finished first on the team and 11th in the league in Statcast's Outs Above Average metric. An elite defender with even elite-r hair, Marisnick glides through Minute Maid Park's spacious center field with ease. He *is* legally required to hit sometimes. This small quirk in the rulebook is what prevents him from being an above-average regular. Teammate Zack Greinke (.240/.281/.346) has an eerily similar line since Marisnick entered the league in 2013, something we can only hope Greinke has pointed out in an Astros group text. Acquired by the Mets in early December, Marisnick will be reunited with Carlos Beltrán as he seeks to take control of the center field job in Flushing.

YEAR	TEAM	LVL	AGE	PA	DRC+	VORP	BABIP	BRR	FRAA	WARP
2017	HOU	MLB	26	259	95	14.4	.320	1.4	CF(93): -5.2, LF(6): 0.3	0.4
2018	FRE	AAA	27	82	164	10.2	.396	-0.5	CF(12): -2.3, RF(6): 0.9	0.6
2018	HOU	MLB	27	235	80	5.9	.292	2.3	CF(96): -5.7, LF(1): 0.0	-0.1
2019	HOU	MLB	28	318	68	-1.5	.310	0.8	CF(109): 7.7	0.7
2020	NYN	MLB	29	322	71	0.8	.272	1.1	CF -1	0.0

Jake Marisnick, continued

Batted Ball Distribution

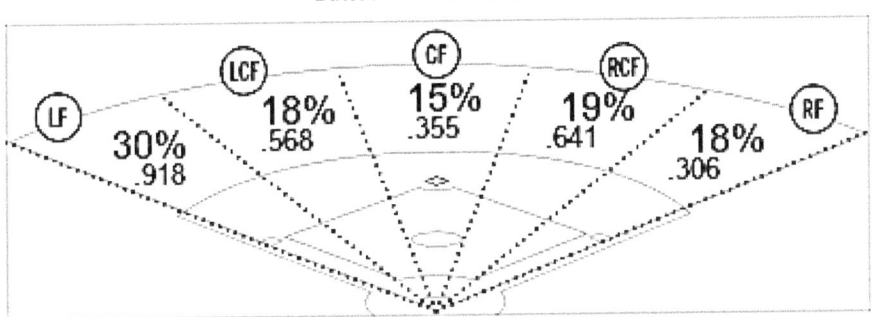

Strike Zone vs LHP   Strike Zone vs RHP

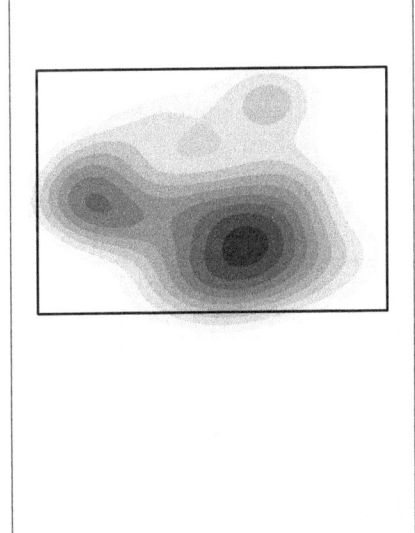

Jeff McNeil 3B/OF

Born: 04/08/92 Age: 28 Bats: L Throws: R
Height: 6'1" Weight: 195 Origin: Round 12, 2013 Draft (#356 overall)

YEAR	TEAM	LVL	AGE	PA	R	2B	3B	HR	RBI	BB	K	SB	CS	AVG/OBP/SLG
2017	SLU	A+	25	116	13	7	0	3	15	7	19	2	2	.324/.388/.476
2017	LVG	AAA	25	78	12	5	0	1	6	3	10	2	0	.254/.295/.366
2018	BIN	AA	26	241	49	16	3	14	43	22	23	3	0	.327/.402/.626
2018	LVG	AAA	26	143	23	10	2	5	28	14	19	3	0	.368/.427/.600
2018	NYN	MLB	26	248	35	11	6	3	19	14	24	7	1	.329/.381/.471
2019	NYN	MLB	27	567	83	38	1	23	75	35	75	5	6	.318/.384/.531
2020	NYN	MLB	28	595	72	28	3	22	79	38	83	8	3	.287/.352/.470

Comparables: Joe Panik, Justin Turner, Vance Law

Two years ago, McNeil was about as far from being a major-league All-Star as a 25-year-old professional baseball player could be. He had barely played in 2016 and 2017 while battling injuries, and had little experience or success above A-ball. He had twice been left unprotected in the Rule 5 Draft and was passed over both times. A bad start in Double-A in 2018 might've gotten him released, but instead McNeil started mashing right out of the gate, hitting his way to the majors by the end of July. He continued mashing throughout 2019 while seeing significant time at four different positions, earning that first All-Star nod and establishing himself as one of baseball's most versatile stars. He even adopted an adorable new puppy, Willow, from a team event with the North Shore Animal League, and Willow McNeil's puppy power sparked newfound power at the plate from her human.

13/10 would let both play in the outfield.

YEAR	TEAM	LVL	AGE	PA	DRC+	VORP	BABIP	BRR	FRAA	WARP
2017	SLU	A+	25	116	165	7.4	.373	-0.6	2B(18): -1.5, 3B(4): -0.3	0.7
2017	LVG	AAA	25	78	74	0.5	.274	1.0	2B(17): 0.2, 3B(1): 0.6	0.2
2018	BIN	AA	26	241	176	31.4	.316	1.7	2B(47): 3.9, 3B(9): -0.6	3.2
2018	LVG	AAA	26	143	152	15.4	.394	0.4	2B(24): -3.3, 3B(3): -0.1	1.1
2018	NYN	MLB	26	248	119	24.4	.359	0.8	2B(54): -2.6, 3B(4): 0.3	1.2
2019	NYN	MLB	27	567	129	38.1	.337	-2.7	LF(71): -5.2, RF(42): -1.2	2.5
2020	NYN	MLB	28	595	117	28.4	.306	-0.6	3B -1, 2B -1	2.5

Jeff McNeil, continued

Batted Ball Distribution

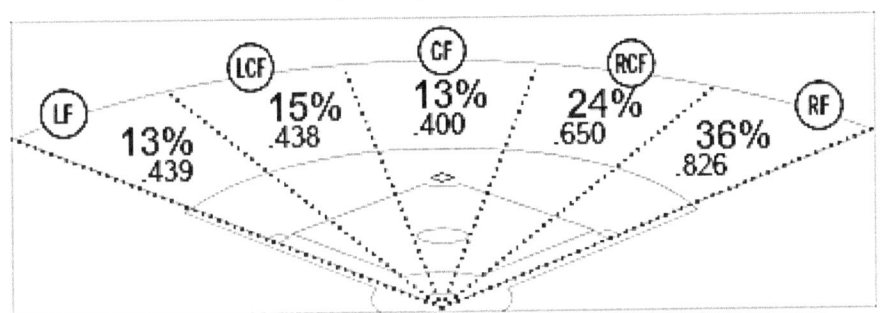

Strike Zone vs LHP   **Strike Zone vs RHP**

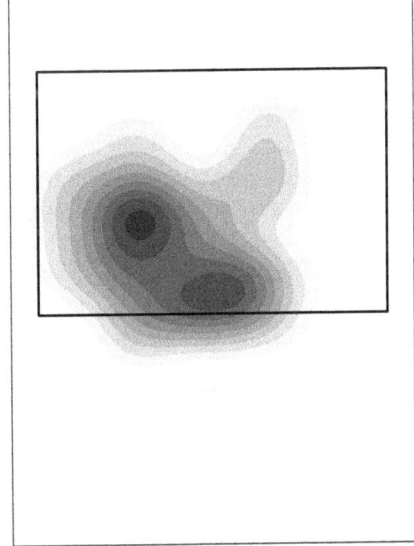

Tomás Nido C

Born: 04/12/94 Age: 26 Bats: R Throws: R
Height: 6'0" Weight: 210 Origin: Round 8, 2012 Draft (#260 overall)

YEAR	TEAM	LVL	AGE	PA	R	2B	3B	HR	RBI	BB	K	SB	CS	AVG/OBP/SLG
2017	BIN	AA	23	404	41	19	1	8	60	30	63	0	0	.232/.287/.354
2017	NYN	MLB	23	10	0	1	0	0	3	0	2	0	0	.300/.300/.400
2018	BIN	AA	24	228	23	18	1	5	30	7	36	0	0	.274/.298/.437
2018	NYN	MLB	24	90	10	3	0	1	9	4	27	0	0	.167/.200/.238
2019	SYR	AAA	25	40	3	1	0	0	4	1	13	0	0	.289/.300/.316
2019	NYN	MLB	25	144	9	5	0	4	14	7	37	0	0	.191/.231/.316
2020	NYN	MLB	26	210	19	11	0	6	22	11	57	0	0	.223/.265/.365

Comparables: John Hicks, A.J. Jimenez, Tucker Barnhart

The Mets saw a need at catcher, addressed it, made a mess of it, forced Devin Mesoraco to retire and ended up with Nido on the Opening Day roster in 2019. For his young major-league career, he has not shown much offensively, and last season was no different. As the season wore on, however, Nido became Noah Syndergaard's personal safety net—which would ultimately become quite the point of consternation down the stretch as the Mets worked their way back into nominal contention. Eventually Mickey Callaway threw everyone for a loop when he cited "catcher wins" as a stat and as a reason Nido lost playing time, even when Syndergaard was pitching. With Callaway gone, Carlos Beltrán and company will have to find their own balance between comfort and contact.

YEAR	TEAM	P. COUNT	FRM RUNS	BLK RUNS	THRW RUNS	TOT RUNS
2017	BIN	10148	27.4	2.3	0.6	30.8
2017	NYN	379	0.1	0.3	0.0	1.7
2018	BIN	6337	7.7	0.0	0.5	8.2
2018	NYN	3444	3.5	-0.1	0.0	3.3
2019	NYN	5589	5.3	0.4	-0.6	5.1
2019	SYR	1196	1.2	0.1	0.1	1.3
2020	NYN	8113	6.5	1.0	-0.4	7.0

YEAR	TEAM	LVL	AGE	PA	DRC+	VORP	BABIP	BRR	FRAA	WARP
2017	BIN	AA	23	404	68	4.0	.255	2.4	C(85): 28.4	3.7
2017	NYN	MLB	23	10	89	0.2	.375	-0.1	C(3): 0.3	0.1
2018	BIN	AA	24	228	112	6.1	.303	-2.0	C(48): 8.5	2.0
2018	NYN	MLB	24	90	58	-3.7	.224	0.2	C(30): 3.4	0.3
2019	SYR	AAA	25	40	79	-0.8	.423	-1.2	C(11): 1.4	0.1
2019	NYN	MLB	25	144	58	-0.4	.232	-1.5	C(48): 5.1	0.3
2020	NYN	MLB	26	210	66	0.1	.284	-0.5	C 7	0.7

Tomás Nido, continued

Batted Ball Distribution

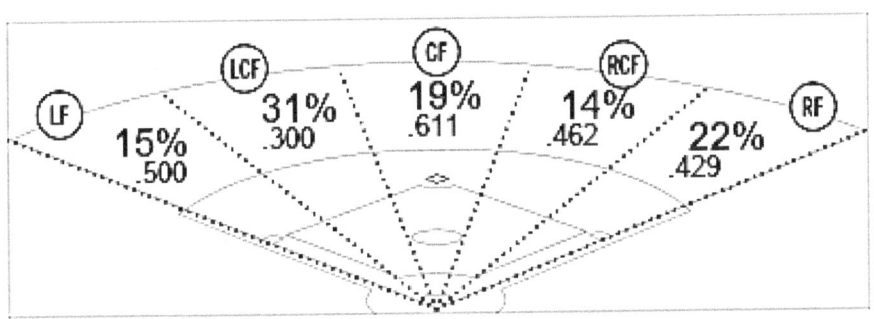

Strike Zone vs LHP   Strike Zone vs RHP

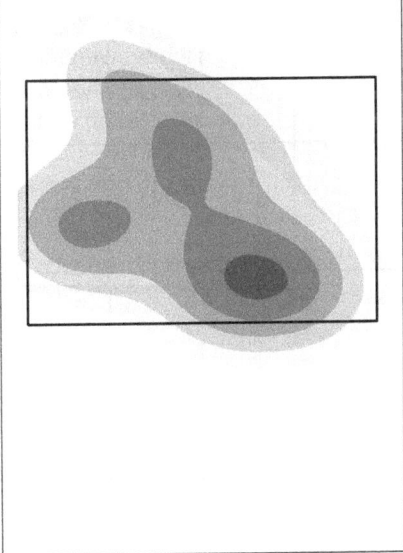

Brandon Nimmo CF

Born: 03/27/93 Age: 27 Bats: L Throws: R
Height: 6'3" Weight: 207 Origin: Round 1, 2011 Draft (#13 overall)

YEAR	TEAM	LVL	AGE	PA	R	2B	3B	HR	RBI	BB	K	SB	CS	AVG/OBP/SLG
2017	LVG	AAA	24	198	23	12	1	3	17	33	49	0	0	.227/.364/.368
2017	NYN	MLB	24	215	26	11	1	5	21	33	60	2	0	.260/.379/.418
2018	NYN	MLB	25	535	77	28	8	17	47	80	140	9	6	.263/.404/.483
2019	SYR	AAA	26	44	10	2	0	1	6	8	8	3	0	.200/.364/.343
2019	NYN	MLB	26	254	34	11	1	8	29	46	71	3	0	.221/.375/.407
2020	NYN	MLB	27	490	59	21	3	15	58	71	129	6	3	.238/.362/.415

Comparables: Dalton Pompey, Aaron Cunningham, Desmond Jennings

The overall season numbers hide a dynamic return for the Happiest Man in Baseball after missing a good chunk of the year with a neck injury. Being wary of September stats is a tried and true tradition, but if you're going to show up once the kids go back to school, you might as well make the most of it. Nimmo certainly did just that with a .430 on-base percentage, five homers and a nearly square strikeout-to-walk rate. It turns out having a healthy neck is instrumental in being able to turn while swinging a bat. His return was an instant boost to the lineup down the stretch, and he worked his way back into the leadoff role where he should return in 2020. As an exclamation point, he walked off a game in the final week of the season in the most Nimmo way possible, with a bases-loaded walk, a signature sprint to first, a bright smile and a plea to Pete Alonso to not rip the jersey. Request denied.

YEAR	TEAM	LVL	AGE	PA	DRC+	VORP	BABIP	BRR	FRAA	WARP
2017	LVG	AAA	24	198	96	5.6	.306	-1.0	CF(31): -4.8, RF(12): 2.2	0.2
2017	NYN	MLB	24	215	92	12.3	.360	-0.9	LF(32): 3.0, CF(12): 0.5	0.6
2018	NYN	MLB	25	535	123	57.0	.351	5.1	RF(62): 0.1, CF(44): -0.9	3.6
2019	SYR	AAA	26	44	101	2.1	.231	0.2	CF(8): 0.4, LF(2): -0.2	0.2
2019	NYN	MLB	26	254	100	8.5	.293	1.0	CF(43): 0.0, LF(37): -0.8	0.9
2020	NYN	MLB	27	490	111	25.5	.310	1.7	CF -1, LF 2	2.9

Brandon Nimmo, continued

Batted Ball Distribution

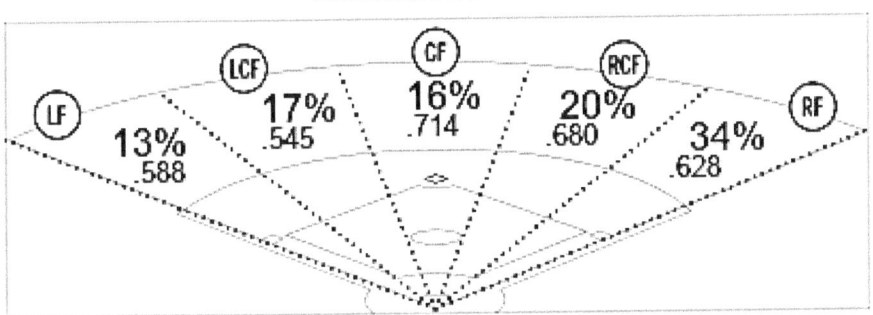

Strike Zone vs LHP   **Strike Zone vs RHP**

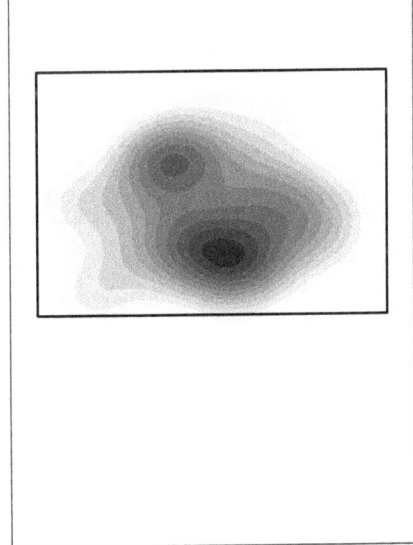

Eduardo Núñez   INF

Born: 06/15/87   Age: 33   Bats: R   Throws: R
Height: 6'0"   Weight: 195   Origin: International Free Agent, 2004

YEAR	TEAM	LVL	AGE	PA	R	2B	3B	HR	RBI	BB	K	SB	CS	AVG/OBP/SLG
2017	SFN	MLB	30	318	37	21	0	4	31	12	29	18	5	.308/.334/.417
2017	BOS	MLB	30	173	23	12	0	8	27	6	25	6	2	.321/.353/.539
2018	BOS	MLB	31	502	56	23	3	10	44	16	69	7	2	.265/.289/.388
2019	BOS	MLB	32	174	13	7	0	2	20	4	27	5	1	.228/.243/.305
2020	BOS	MLB	33	251	24	12	1	5	26	10	41	9	3	.254/.289/.381

Comparables: Charlie Hayes, Hubie Brooks, Martín Prado

Harken back to the halcyon days of Núñez's career. What comes to mind? Perhaps it's speed; Núñez stole 24 bases as recently as 2017. Maybe it's versatility? Núñez has more than 150 appearances each at second base, third base and shortstop in his career, as well as 50-plus more in the outfield. Maybe you recall the way Núñez's bat would randomly catch fire, especially against left-handed pitching? It's best to cling to those happy memories, because the Núñez of the present—the one whom the Sox released in July and whom no other team even took a flier on—looks cooked. He can't run. He hit .200/.240/.313 against southpaws. And let's be real, he could never really field. Rumors of Núñez's demise have been greatly exaggerated before, but they've never come as Núñez was a 32-year-old with a long history of leg injuries.

YEAR	TEAM	LVL	AGE	PA	DRC+	VORP	BABIP	BRR	FRAA	WARP
2017	SFN	MLB	30	318	104	18.3	.328	4.4	3B(49): -0.1, LF(19): 2.3	1.8
2017	BOS	MLB	30	173	105	11.9	.341	-1.2	2B(26): -0.8, SS(5): 0.0	0.5
2018	BOS	MLB	31	502	84	-1.3	.290	-2.6	2B(74): -2.0, 3B(45): 1.2	0.2
2019	BOS	MLB	32	174	59	-3.9	.257	1.7	2B(31): 1.3, 3B(8): -0.5	-0.2
2020	BOS	MLB	33	251	76	0.4	.287	0.2	2B -1, 3B 0	0.0

Eduardo Núñez, continued

Batted Ball Distribution

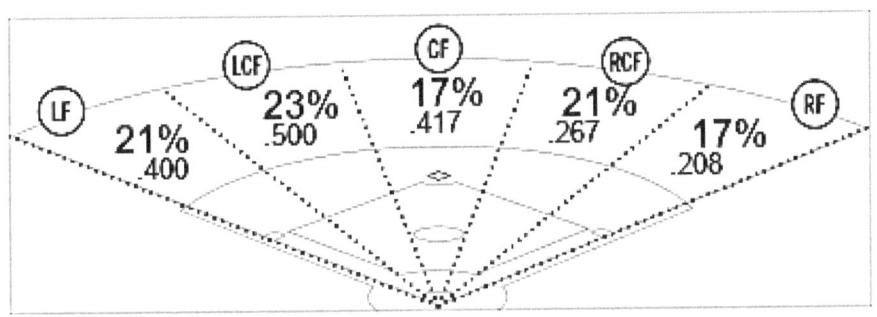

Strike Zone vs LHP Strike Zone vs RHP

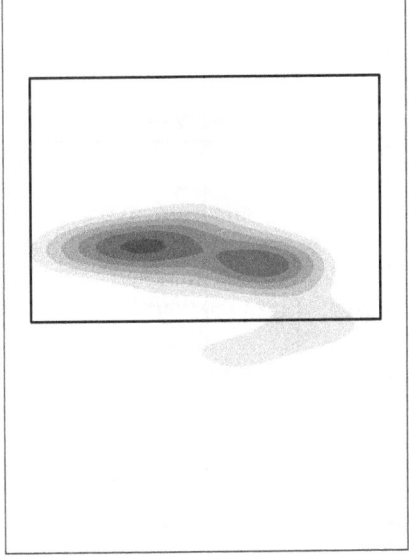

Wilson Ramos C

Born: 08/10/87 Age: 32 Bats: R Throws: R
Height: 6'1" Weight: 245 Origin: International Free Agent, 2004

YEAR	TEAM	LVL	AGE	PA	R	2B	3B	HR	RBI	BB	K	SB	CS	AVG/OBP/SLG
2017	DUR	AAA	29	30	4	2	0	2	5	2	1	0	0	.250/.300/.536
2017	TBA	MLB	29	224	19	6	0	11	35	10	36	0	0	.260/.290/.447
2018	TBA	MLB	30	315	30	14	0	14	53	22	61	0	0	.297/.346/.488
2018	PHI	MLB	30	101	9	8	1	1	17	10	19	0	0	.337/.396/.483
2019	NYN	MLB	31	524	52	19	0	14	73	44	69	1	0	.288/.351/.416
2020	NYN	MLB	32	483	51	21	0	15	57	33	78	1	0	.263/.316/.412

Comparables: Rod Barajas, Ramon Hernandez, Josh Bard

YEAR	TEAM	P. COUNT	FRM RUNS	BLK RUNS	THRW RUNS	TOT RUNS
2017	TBA	8203	1.4	-3.9	-0.8	-4.1
2018	TBA	9850	0.2	0.3	-0.2	0.6
2018	PHI	3106	0.1	-0.3	0.2	0.3
2019	NYN	17231	-4.7	-0.5	-3.3	-8.6
2020	NYN	22300	0.1	-1.4	-3.1	-4.3

The Mets had an uncertain-at-best catching situation develop prior to the 2019 season with Travis d'Arnaud recovering from Tommy John surgery and their two backups, Kevin Plawecki and Tomás Nido, barely owning bats. GM Brodie Van Wagenen addressed the problem when he signed Ramos to be their primary backstop. Offensively, the signing ended up working out well after it was touch-and-go for the first few months. Defensively, the signing was a mess. Ramos threw himself fully into bad framer territory, the final chapter of a precipitous decline from his early-decade peak. Despite losing the confidence of some of the starting staff and sitting on a .709 OPS at the end of July, Mickey Callaway stuck with him and he subsequently went on a tear. During the Mets charge back into the Wild Card race, Ramos had a 26-game hit streak and hit .347/.392/.485 between August and September. In fact, he was playing with so much house money that he even stole the first base of his career off former Met Anthony Swarzak.

YEAR	TEAM	LVL	AGE	PA	DRC+	VORP	BABIP	BRR	FRAA	WARP
2017	DUR	AAA	29	30	109	0.9	.200	-0.2	C(6): 0.3	0.1
2017	TBA	MLB	29	224	101	4.1	.262	-3.4	C(62): -3.1	0.5
2018	TBA	MLB	30	315	121	15.6	.335	-4.4	C(73): -0.8	1.8
2018	PHI	MLB	30	101	123	8.4	.408	-2.6	C(23): 0.0	0.5
2019	NYN	MLB	31	524	100	27.2	.310	-4.6	C(124): -6.7	1.6
2020	NYN	MLB	32	483	95	14.4	.290	-5.0	C -4	1.1

Wilson Ramos, continued

Batted Ball Distribution

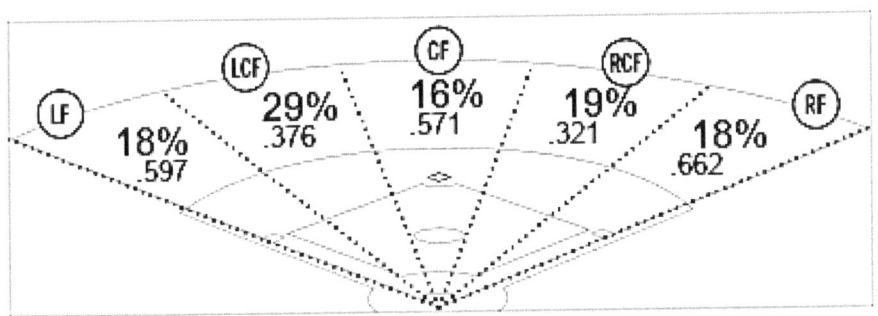

Strike Zone vs LHP   **Strike Zone vs RHP**

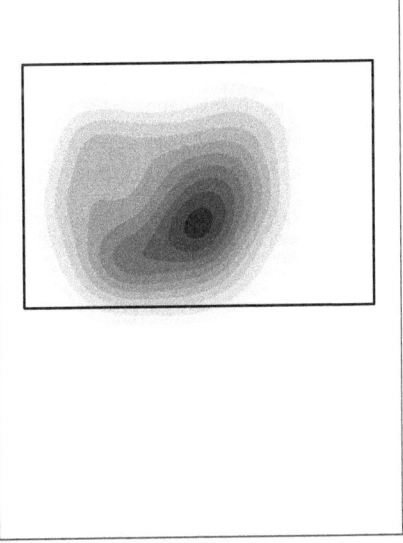

Amed Rosario SS

Born: 11/20/95 Age: 24 Bats: R Throws: R
Height: 6'2" Weight: 189 Origin: International Free Agent, 2012

YEAR	TEAM	LVL	AGE	PA	R	2B	3B	HR	RBI	BB	K	SB	CS	AVG/OBP/SLG
2017	LVG	AAA	21	425	66	19	7	7	58	23	67	19	6	.328/.367/.466
2017	NYN	MLB	21	170	16	4	4	4	10	3	49	7	3	.248/.271/.394
2018	NYN	MLB	22	592	76	26	8	9	51	29	119	24	11	.256/.295/.381
2019	NYN	MLB	23	655	75	30	7	15	72	31	124	19	10	.287/.323/.432
2020	NYN	MLB	24	595	57	27	5	12	62	29	119	16	6	.259/.300/.392

Comparables: Chris Owings, Wilmer Flores, Orlando Arcia

After whispers of "bust" followed Rosario as he scuffled for most of his sophomore season, he took major steps forward offensively in his third campaign. Unfortunately for the 24-year-old, it still left him as a below-average hitter despite leading all National League shortstops in hits. A player's WARP is supposed to be the sum of his strengths, but for Rosario it sits as a reminder of what stands between him and the stardom that was promised when he was a prospect. He hits for contact, but is overaggressive at the plate and is nearly allergic to walks. He plays a premium defensive position, but he can't do it at a high enough level to ward off talks of a move to center field. He uses his speed to steal bases, but he also gets caught nearly a third of the time. The transition from what Rosario could do to what he can't do is approaching, and his assignment is laid bare in front of him.

YEAR	TEAM	LVL	AGE	PA	DRC+	VORP	BABIP	BRR	FRAA	WARP
2017	LVG	AAA	21	425	115	31.3	.377	1.4	SS(88): 2.0, 3B(6): -0.2	3.0
2017	NYN	MLB	21	170	69	0.6	.330	1.0	SS(45): -0.3	0.2
2018	NYN	MLB	22	592	83	22.6	.310	2.8	SS(146): -6.6	1.0
2019	NYN	MLB	23	655	96	28.2	.338	1.5	SS(152): -6.0, LF(1): -0.1	2.3
2020	NYN	MLB	24	595	86	14.1	.309	2.2	SS -4	1.0

Amed Rosario, continued

Batted Ball Distribution

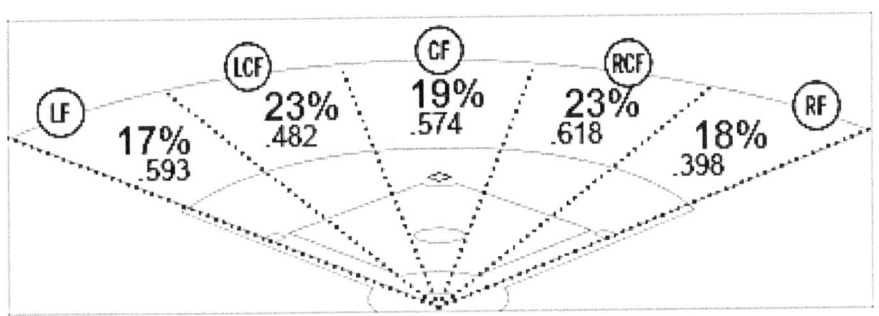

Strike Zone vs LHP

Strike Zone vs RHP

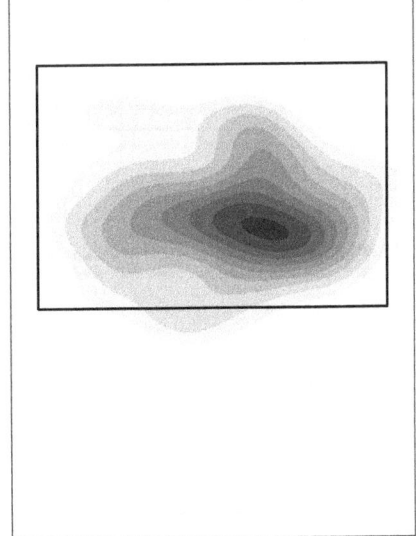

Dominic Smith 1B

Born: 06/15/95   Age: 25   Bats: L   Throws: L
Height: 6'0"   Weight: 239   Origin: Round 1, 2013 Draft (#11 overall)

YEAR	TEAM	LVL	AGE	PA	R	2B	3B	HR	RBI	BB	K	SB	CS	AVG/OBP/SLG
2017	LVG	AAA	22	500	77	34	2	16	76	39	87	1	1	.330/.386/.519
2017	NYN	MLB	22	183	17	6	0	9	26	14	49	0	0	.198/.262/.395
2018	LVG	AAA	23	375	52	21	1	6	41	34	76	3	0	.258/.328/.380
2018	NYN	MLB	23	149	14	11	1	5	11	4	47	0	0	.224/.255/.420
2019	NYN	MLB	24	197	35	10	0	11	25	19	44	1	2	.282/.355/.525
2020	NYN	MLB	25	175	19	7	0	7	22	14	41	0	0	.241/.304/.416

Comparables: Ronald Guzmán, Steve Bilko, Cecil Fielder

Smith and his injured foot became legendary whenever he was spotted taking his scooter for a ride on the field after big wins. His presence may have still been felt in the clubhouse while he was out with a stress reaction in his foot, but his lefty bat in the midst of a breakout season was missed off the bench. Finding a cure for sleep apnea helped contribute to his meteoric rise with the bat, yet Smith had trouble finding a spot on the field with a soon-to-be Rookie of the Year entrenched at his natural position. Left field was a bridge too far, even for a team that openly sacrificed defense for offense throughout the year. However, he took his legend to a new level on the final day of the regular season. After not being able to play for two months, he strode to the plate with two out in the bottom of the 11th inning and the Mets down two. A three-run homer and complete pandemonium at Citi Field ensued.

YEAR	TEAM	LVL	AGE	PA	DRC+	VORP	BABIP	BRR	FRAA	WARP
2017	LVG	AAA	22	500	128	24.0	.380	-2.4	1B(107): 6.6	2.8
2017	NYN	MLB	22	183	80	-3.3	.218	0.3	1B(46): -5.5	-0.7
2018	LVG	AAA	23	375	83	3.6	.315	1.9	1B(53): 6.5, LF(22): -0.2	1.0
2018	NYN	MLB	23	149	77	1.1	.297	0.3	1B(28): -0.5, LF(13): -1.9	-0.4
2019	NYN	MLB	24	197	112	8.3	.320	2.8	1B(36): -0.6, LF(32): -1.0	0.9
2020	NYN	MLB	25	175	89	3.1	.284	0.9	LF 0, 1B 1	0.4

Dominic Smith, continued

Batted Ball Distribution

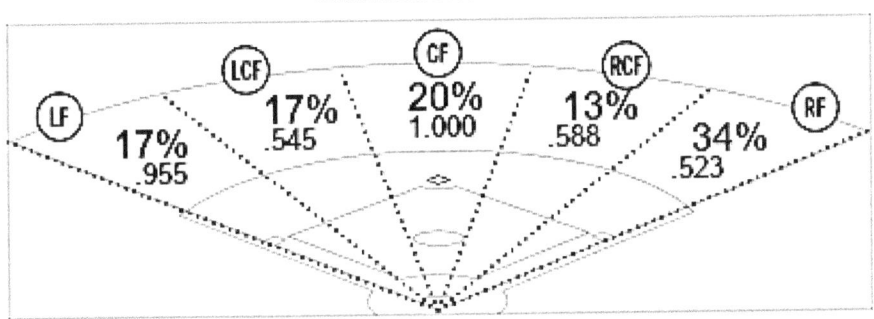

Strike Zone vs LHP

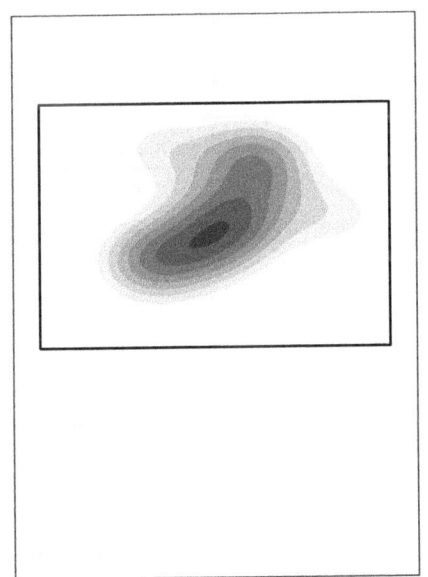

Strike Zone vs RHP

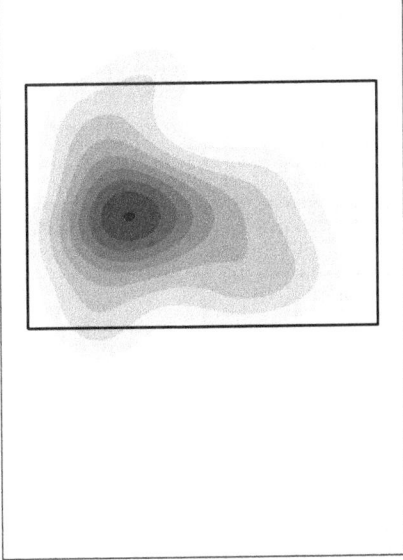

Brad Brach RHP

Born: 04/12/86 Age: 34 Bats: R Throws: R
Height: 6'6" Weight: 215 Origin: Round 42, 2008 Draft (#1275 overall)

YEAR	TEAM	LVL	AGE	W	L	SV	G	GS	IP	H	HR	BB/9	K/9	K	GB%	BABIP
2017	BAL	MLB	31	4	5	18	67	0	68	51	7	3.4	9.3	70	42%	.256
2018	BAL	MLB	32	1	2	11	42	0	39	50	4	4.4	8.8	38	48%	.371
2018	ATL	MLB	32	1	2	1	27	0	23^2	22	1	3.4	8.4	22	47%	.296
2019	CHN	MLB	33	4	3	0	42	0	39^2	42	3	6.4	10.2	45	39%	.375
2019	NYN	MLB	33	1	1	0	16	0	14^2	15	1	1.8	9.2	15	40%	.333
2020	NYN	MLB	34	2	2	0	40	0	43	38	6	3.9	9.8	47	42%	.295

Comparables: Steve Cishek, Pedro Strop, Nate Jones

Brach was a sweet addition to the bullpen after he was released by the Cubs in August. He immediately endeared himself to the Queens faithful when he said he grew up a Mets fan and was present at Citi Field for David Wright's home run in the 2015 World Series. After joining the team, he significantly cut down on the walks that plagued him in Chicago and it helped him establish himself as a key member of the bullpen down the stretch. He didn't totally rediscover his All-Star form that he had with the Orioles though, and he continued to get rocked by lefties—his 1.139 OPS against was more of a cry for help than a baseball stat. Much like the candy corn whose name he bears, Brach is good only in small doses. Also, he rocks the orange.

YEAR	TEAM	LVL	AGE	WHIP	ERA	DRA	WARP	MPH	FB%	WHF	CSP
2017	BAL	MLB	31	1.13	3.18	3.39	1.3	96.8	62.9	12.9	46.6
2018	BAL	MLB	32	1.77	4.85	4.28	0.3	95.6	61.4	14	44.5
2018	ATL	MLB	32	1.31	1.52	3.37	0.4	96.2	52.4	13.7	41.6
2019	CHN	MLB	33	1.76	6.13	5.36	0.0	95.8	59.5	13.1	44.5
2019	NYN	MLB	33	1.23	3.68	3.78	0.2	95.5	59.5	12.9	53.8
2020	NYN	MLB	34	1.32	3.90	4.11	0.6	94.9	59	13.1	44.8

Brad Brach, continued

Pitch Shape vs LHH

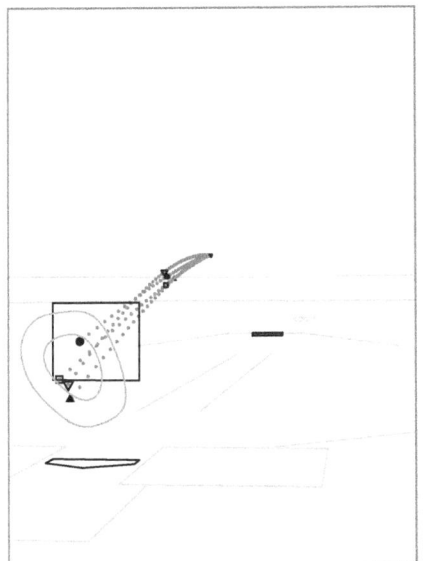

Pitch Shape vs RHH

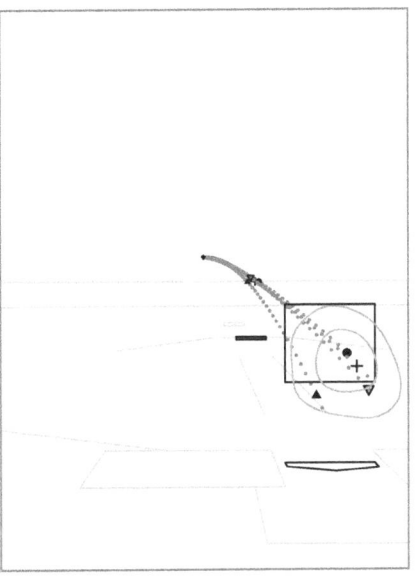

Type	Frequency	Velocity	H Movement	V Movement
● Fastball	48.5%	94.3 [105]	-6 [104]	-15.4 [101]
☐ Sinker	5.4%	92.7 [101]	-12.4 [101]	-20.2 [101]
+ Cutter	8.8%	90.7 [113]	2.6 [104]	-21.9 [108]
▲ Changeup	18.8%	86.7 [105]	-12.1 [95]	-32.3 [86]
✕ Splitter				
▽ Slider	18.4%	85.4 [104]	6 [104]	-32.4 [102]
◇ Curveball				
✦ Slow Curveball				
✱ Knuckleball				
▼ Screwball				

New York Mets 2020

Edwin Díaz RHP

Born: 03/22/94 Age: 26 Bats: R Throws: R
Height: 6'3" Weight: 165 Origin: Round 3, 2012 Draft (#98 overall)

YEAR	TEAM	LVL	AGE	W	L	SV	G	GS	IP	H	HR	BB/9	K/9	K	GB%	BABIP
2017	SEA	MLB	23	4	6	34	66	0	66	44	10	4.4	12.1	89	41%	.236
2018	SEA	MLB	24	0	4	57	73	0	73¹	41	5	2.1	15.2	124	47%	.281
2019	NYN	MLB	25	2	7	26	66	0	58	58	15	3.4	15.4	99	37%	.377
2020	NYN	MLB	26	3	2	30	50	0	53	38	7	3.4	14.6	87	40%	.305

Comparables: Dennis Santana, Nick Kingham, Touki Toussaint

Every great magic trick consists of three parts or acts. The first part is called "The Pledge." The magician shows you something ordinary: an elite strikeout rate, a fastball that touched triple digits or a devastating slider. He shows you these objects. Perhaps he uses them to lead the league in saves to see if it is indeed real, unaltered, normal. But of course...it probably isn't. The second act is called "The Turn." The magician takes the ordinary something and makes it do something extraordinary. Now you're looking for the reasons...but you won't find them, because of course you're not really looking. You don't really want to know. You want to be fooled. But you wouldn't clap yet. Because making something disappear isn't enough; you have to bring it back. That's why every magic trick has a third act, the hardest part, the part we call "The Prestige."

YEAR	TEAM	LVL	AGE	WHIP	ERA	DRA	WARP	MPH	FB%	WHF	CSP
2017	SEA	MLB	23	1.15	3.27	3.20	1.5	100.0	68.4	16.7	46
2018	SEA	MLB	24	0.79	1.96	1.77	2.7	99.8	62.4	20.7	48.4
2019	NYN	MLB	25	1.38	5.59	2.95	1.5	99.9	66.1	19.5	47.1
2020	NYN	MLB	26	1.09	2.84	3.10	1.3	99.5	66.6	19.5	48.1

Edwin Díaz, continued

Pitch Shape vs LHH

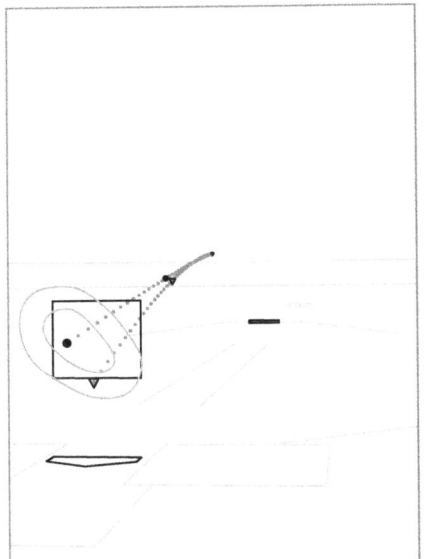

Pitch Shape vs RHH

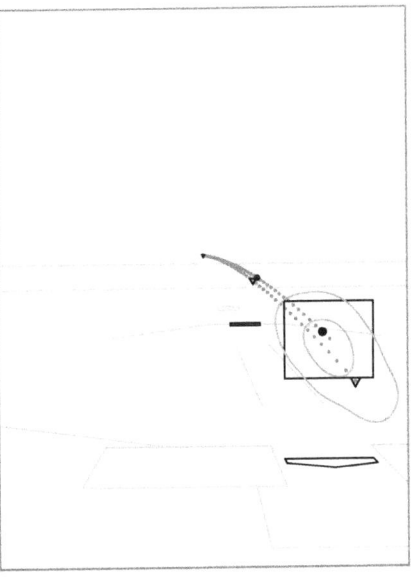

Type	Frequency	Velocity	H Movement	V Movement
● Fastball	65.3%	97.8 [115]	-10.8 [83]	-12.9 [108]
□ Sinker				
+ Cutter				
▲ Changeup				
✕ Splitter				
▽ Slider	33.9%	89.8 [123]	1.6 [86]	-25.3 [123]
◇ Curveball				
⊕ Slow Curveball				
✳ Knuckleball				
▼ Screwball				

Mets Player Analysis - 53

Jeurys Familia   RHP

Born: 10/10/89   Age: 30   Bats: R   Throws: R
Height: 6'3"   Weight: 240   Origin: International Free Agent, 2007

YEAR	TEAM	LVL	AGE	W	L	SV	G	GS	IP	H	HR	BB/9	K/9	K	GB%	BABIP
2017	NYN	MLB	27	2	2	6	26	0	24²	21	1	5.5	9.1	25	61%	.290
2018	NYN	MLB	28	4	4	17	40	0	40²	36	1	3.1	9.5	43	52%	.315
2018	OAK	MLB	28	4	2	1	30	0	31¹	24	2	4.0	11.5	40	40%	.293
2019	NYN	MLB	29	4	2	0	66	0	60	62	7	6.3	9.4	63	52%	.346
2020	NYN	MLB	30	2	2	0	45	0	48	41	5	4.2	9.8	52	52%	.288

Comparables: Kelvin Herrera, Jeremy Jeffress, Luis Avilán

The Mets and Familia reunited in 2019 and it did not feel so good. Unfairly blamed for the 2015 World Series, the right-hander did nothing to alleviate the anxiety from those ill-fated appearances and put together the worst full season of his career. A shoulder injury sidelined him twice in the first half of the season, but his 3.90 ERA after returning from his second IL trip looked a lot less ghastly even if his walk rate was as terrible as ever. When he was traded away in 2018, the return was underwhelming to say the least (sorry, Will Toffey) but at least he was gone. With two years and over $23 million remaining on his contract, the Mets have to be counting down the days until he is once again.

YEAR	TEAM	LVL	AGE	WHIP	ERA	DRA	WARP	MPH	FB%	WHF	CSP
2017	NYN	MLB	27	1.46	4.38	6.48	-0.4	98.4	82.5	10.8	46.6
2018	NYN	MLB	28	1.23	2.88	4.62	0.1	98.3	70.2	12.6	49.6
2018	OAK	MLB	28	1.21	3.45	3.06	0.7	98.9	66.8	17.5	47.3
2019	NYN	MLB	29	1.73	5.70	5.87	-0.3	98.0	66.5	11.9	46.5
2020	NYN	MLB	30	1.31	3.63	3.82	0.8	97.5	69	13	47.1

Jeurys Familia, continued

Pitch Shape vs LHH

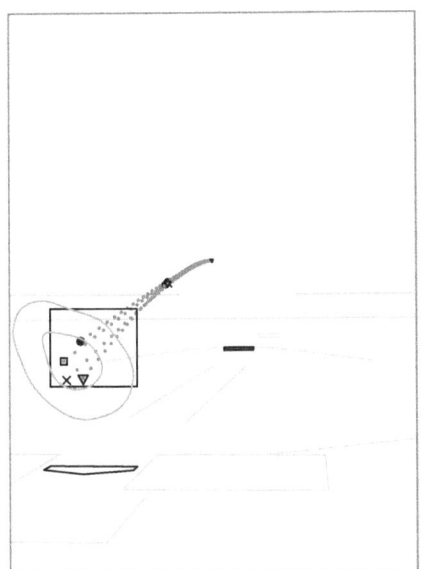

Pitch Shape vs RHH

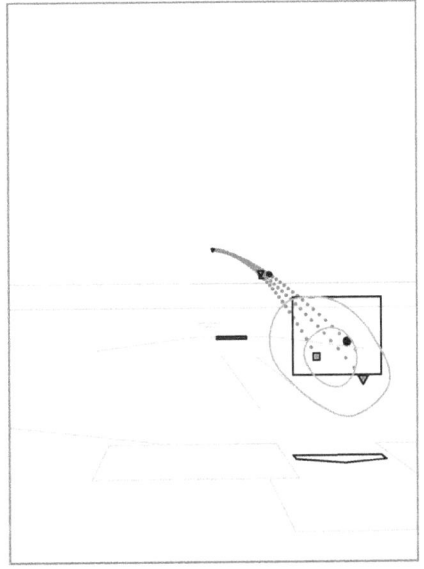

Type	Frequency	Velocity	H Movement	V Movement
● Fastball	17.6%	95.8 [110]	-8.6 [92]	-15.6 [101]
☐ Sinker	48.9%	96.1 [118]	-15 [85]	-21.1 [97]
+ Cutter				
▲ Changeup				
✕ Splitter	7.7%	92.6 [132]	-12.1 [85]	-26 [111]
▽ Slider	25.8%	88.3 [117]	0.5 [81]	-27.1 [117]
◇ Curveball				
⊕ Slow Curveball				
✳ Knuckleball				
▼ Screwball				

Chris Flexen   RHP

Born: 07/01/94   Age: 25   Bats: R   Throws: R
Height: 6'3"   Weight: 250   Origin: Round 14, 2012 Draft (#440 overall)

YEAR	TEAM	LVL	AGE	W	L	SV	G	GS	IP	H	HR	BB/9	K/9	K	GB%	BABIP
2017	SLU	A+	22	0	0	0	3	3	12^2	12	1	2.1	9.2	13	54%	.306
2017	BIN	AA	22	6	1	0	7	7	48^2	28	4	1.3	9.2	50	55%	.203
2017	NYN	MLB	22	3	6	0	14	9	48	62	11	6.6	6.8	36	42%	.342
2018	LVG	AAA	23	6	7	0	18	17	92	109	11	3.0	7.6	78	43%	.354
2018	NYN	MLB	23	0	2	0	4	1	6^1	14	2	8.5	4.3	3	40%	.429
2019	SYR	AAA	24	5	3	0	26	14	78^2	94	11	2.4	10.5	92	46%	.379
2019	NYN	MLB	24	0	3	0	9	1	13^2	15	1	8.6	6.6	10	34%	.304
2020	NYN	MLB	25	2	2	0	33	0	35	36	6	3.7	6.1	24	41%	.278

Comparables: Jackson Stephens, Raúl Alcántara, Zack Littell

Flexen came into camp 30 pounds lighter and tried to flex his muscles out of the bullpen to varying degrees of effectiveness with the big-league club. It is a small sample but a 4.82 ERA as a reliever was actually an improvement for him, compared with a 10.38 ERA as a starter, and if given more of a chance he would have been in higher standing than some of the other Quad-A arms the Mets paraded through the beleaguered bullpen. Instead, he will look to shrink that ERA for the Doosan Bears in the KBO.

YEAR	TEAM	LVL	AGE	WHIP	ERA	DRA	WARP	MPH	FB%	WHF	CSP
2017	SLU	A+	22	1.18	2.13	4.21	0.2				
2017	BIN	AA	22	0.72	1.66	2.03	1.8				
2017	NYN	MLB	22	2.02	7.88	7.82	-1.2	95.1	60.5	8.8	45.9
2018	LVG	AAA	23	1.52	4.40	4.75	0.8				
2018	NYN	MLB	23	3.16	12.79	7.44	-0.2	94.6	62.3	6	45
2019	SYR	AAA	24	1.46	4.46	5.34	1.0				
2019	NYN	MLB	24	2.05	6.59	6.03	-0.1	96.8	61.7	8.4	46.8
2020	NYN	MLB	25	1.44	5.00	5.16	0.1	95.2	62.5	8.5	47.1

Chris Flexen, continued

Pitch Shape vs LHH

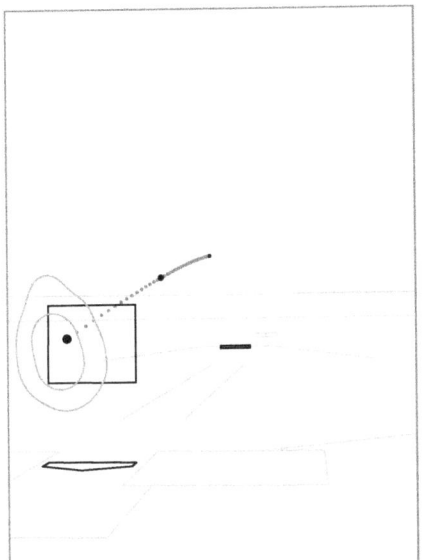

Pitch Shape vs RHH

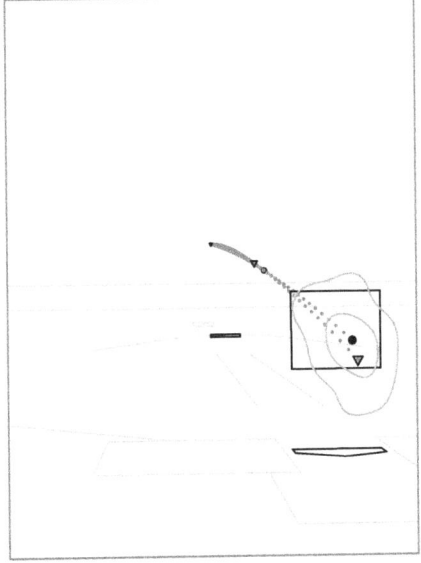

Type	Frequency	Velocity	H Movement	V Movement
● Fastball	58.8%	94.6 [106]	-4.5 [110]	-12.4 [109]
☐ Sinker				
+ Cutter				
▲ Changeup	12.8%	83.9 [95]	-9.8 [106]	-28.6 [96]
✕ Splitter				
▽ Slider	21.9%	88.4 [117]	4.8 [99]	-27 [118]
◇ Curveball	3.6%	78.3 [99]	6.7 [97]	-51.6 [91]
⊕ Slow Curveball				
✳ Knuckleball				
▼ Screwball				

Robert Gsellman   RHP

Born: 07/18/93 Age: 26 Bats: R Throws: R
Height: 6'4" Weight: 205 Origin: Round 13, 2011 Draft (#402 overall)

YEAR	TEAM	LVL	AGE	W	L	SV	G	GS	IP	H	HR	BB/9	K/9	K	GB%	BABIP
2017	BIN	AA	23	1	0	0	4	4	12¹	15	0	3.6	6.6	9	76%	.366
2017	LVG	AAA	23	0	0	0	1	1	6	10	1	4.5	4.5	3	50%	.391
2017	NYN	MLB	23	8	7	0	25	22	119²	138	17	3.2	6.2	82	51%	.303
2018	NYN	MLB	24	6	3	13	68	0	80	76	8	3.2	7.9	70	52%	.291
2019	NYN	MLB	25	2	3	1	52	0	63²	64	7	3.3	8.5	60	45%	.315
2020	NYN	MLB	26	3	3	0	55	0	59	55	7	3.3	8.0	52	49%	.284

Comparables: Sal Romano, Zack Littell, Wade Davis

Gsellman was one of the few relievers who unequivocally gained entry into Mickey Callaway's circle of trust, which led to both a mixed bag of results and heavy usage that ultimately led to a season-ending injury. He also ended 2019 with one of the most bizarre home/road splits. Gsellman gave up six of his seven homers on road, and yet he pitched to a 2.29 ERA. On the other hand, the former top prospect got absolutely BABIP'd to death at Citi Field and that .449 mark led to a brutal 8.51 ERA at home. Gsellman remains as much of an enigma as that split, someone who is capable of appearing dominant at times but is just as likely to be a low-key adventure on the mound.

YEAR	TEAM	LVL	AGE	WHIP	ERA	DRA	WARP	MPH	FB%	WHF	CSP
2017	BIN	AA	23	1.62	2.92	5.67	-0.1				
2017	LVG	AAA	23	2.17	7.50	7.78	-0.1				
2017	NYN	MLB	23	1.50	5.19	5.77	-0.3	95.2	63.4	8.1	45.7
2018	NYN	MLB	24	1.30	4.28	4.38	0.5	96.6	62.8	10.8	49.3
2019	NYN	MLB	25	1.37	4.66	4.85	0.3	97.3	51.8	12.3	47
2020	NYN	MLB	26	1.30	4.01	4.24	0.8	95.9	60.5	10.5	48.3

Robert Gsellman, continued

Pitch Shape vs LHH

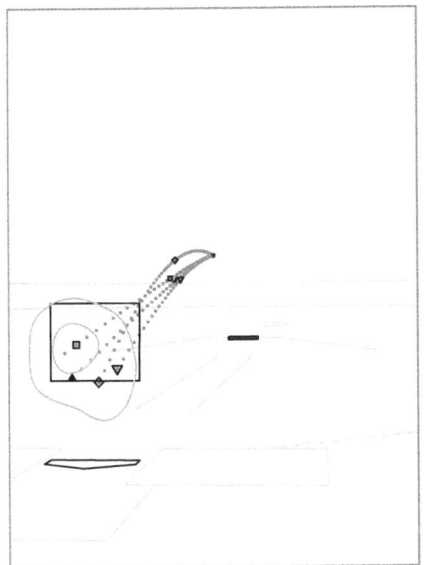

Pitch Shape vs RHH

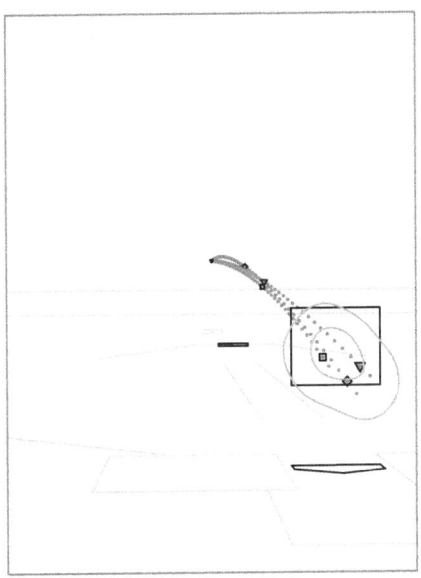

Type	Frequency	Velocity	H Movement	V Movement
● Fastball	3.6%	95.7 [109]	-10.2 [85]	-13.1 [107]
▢ Sinker	48.1%	95.6 [115]	-14.2 [90]	-17 [112]
+ Cutter				
▲ Changeup	10.0%	87.6 [108]	-12.9 [92]	-22.5 [114]
✕ Splitter				
▽ Slider	26.5%	90.7 [127]	-0.7 [76]	-25.2 [123]
◇ Curveball	11.7%	81.5 [110]	10.6 [113]	-47.6 [100]
⬥ Slow Curveball				
✱ Knuckleball				
▼ Screwball				

Seth Lugo RHP

Born: 11/17/89   Age: 30   Bats: R   Throws: R
Height: 6'4"   Weight: 225   Origin: Round 34, 2011 Draft (#1032 overall)

YEAR	TEAM	LVL	AGE	W	L	SV	G	GS	IP	H	HR	BB/9	K/9	K	GB%	BABIP
2017	SLU	A+	27	0	1	0	2	1	6^2	9	2	1.4	5.4	4	48%	.304
2017	BIN	AA	27	1	1	0	2	2	13	14	1	1.4	10.4	15	54%	.382
2017	NYN	MLB	27	7	5	0	19	18	101^1	114	13	2.2	7.5	85	43%	.325
2018	NYN	MLB	28	3	4	3	54	5	101^1	81	9	2.5	9.1	103	47%	.269
2019	NYN	MLB	29	7	4	6	61	0	80	56	8	1.8	11.7	104	44%	.265
2020	NYN	MLB	30	3	3	9	55	0	59	51	8	2.4	10.2	67	44%	.292

Comparables: Chase Whitley, Chris Leroux, Andrew Triggs

After coming down with an illness early in the season, Lugo came back more dominant than ever and morphed into Seth Flugo, the man with downright nasty stuff and poor puns. Known for his sick curveball and its dizzying spin rate, it caused quite a few headaches for batters last season. With a UCL on double-secret probation, his usage had to be monitored, but he was able to both stay healthy for a full season and turn into an otherworldly force in the second half of the season. From July 1 on, Lugo had a 1.80 ERA, 0.60 WHIP and a preposterous 51 strikeouts against only four walks, all while pitching in the most high-leverage situations possible during a playoff run. The self-proclaimed Quarterrican (in honor of his paternal grandfather) was one of the few bright spots in the infectious disaster that was the Mets' 2019 bullpen, and he looked so out of place that the Mets once again are discussing a potential move into the rotation.

YEAR	TEAM	LVL	AGE	WHIP	ERA	DRA	WARP	MPH	FB%	WHF	CSP
2017	SLU	A+	27	1.50	8.10	5.83	-0.1				
2017	BIN	AA	27	1.23	2.77	3.77	0.2				
2017	NYN	MLB	27	1.37	4.71	5.26	0.3	94.3	56.8	9.7	50.3
2018	NYN	MLB	28	1.08	2.66	3.82	1.4	97.0	48.8	10.8	50
2019	NYN	MLB	29	0.90	2.70	2.71	2.3	96.9	56.7	12.2	51.3
2020	NYN	MLB	30	1.14	3.24	3.55	1.2	95.5	53.7	11	50.4

Seth Lugo, continued

Pitch Shape vs LHH

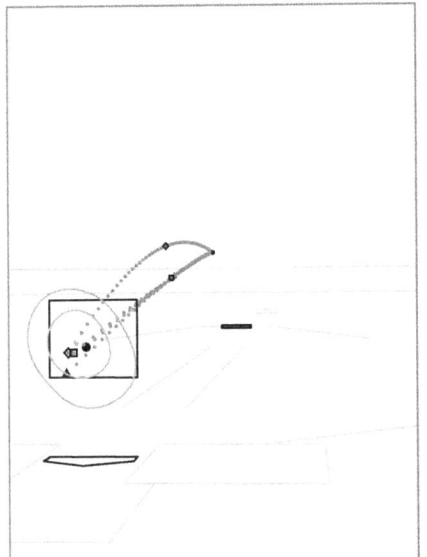

Pitch Shape vs RHH

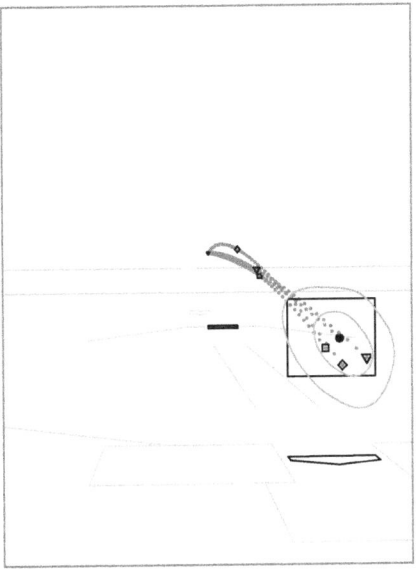

Type	Frequency	Velocity	H Movement	V Movement
● Fastball	35.0%	94.8 [107]	-6.3 [102]	-12.7 [108]
☐ Sinker	21.7%	94.3 [109]	-13.7 [93]	-17 [112]
+ Cutter				
▲ Changeup	6.7%	88.3 [111]	-13 [92]	-23.5 [111]
✕ Splitter				
▽ Slider	13.0%	88.3 [116]	3.5 [94]	-25.4 [122]
◇ Curveball	23.6%	79.8 [104]	11.6 [117]	-54.1 [86]
⊕ Slow Curveball				
✳ Knuckleball				
▼ Screwball				

Mets Player Analysis - 61

Steven Matz   LHP
Born: 05/29/91   Age: 29   Bats: R   Throws: L
Height: 6'2"   Weight: 200   Origin: Round 2, 2009 Draft (#72 overall)

YEAR	TEAM	LVL	AGE	W	L	SV	G	GS	IP	H	HR	BB/9	K/9	K	GB%	BABIP
2017	LVG	AAA	26	0	1	0	3	3	13¹	13	3	1.4	11.5	17	35%	.323
2017	NYN	MLB	26	2	7	0	13	13	66²	83	12	2.6	6.5	48	49%	.329
2018	NYN	MLB	27	5	11	0	30	30	154	134	25	3.4	8.9	152	50%	.267
2019	NYN	MLB	28	11	10	0	32	30	160¹	163	27	2.9	8.6	153	48%	.301
2020	NYN	MLB	29	7	6	0	21	21	107	102	17	2.7	8.3	99	48%	.283

Comparables: Drew Smyly, Andrew Heaney, Jordan Montgomery

"I learned to recognise the thorough and primitive duality of man; I saw that, of the two natures that contended in the field of my consciousness, even if I could rightly be said to be either, it was only because I was radically both." Robert Louis Stevenson's words described the main character(s) in his famous novel, *The Strange Case of Dr. Jekyll and Mr. Hyde*, but he might as well have written it about the enigmatic Matz. Nobody had more pronounced and prolonged home/road splits than the southpaw. At home, he had a lower ERA than Jacob deGrom. On the road, he had a higher ERA than Jeurys Familia. After holding him back to face the Marlins at home rather than the Reds on the road with a week left in the regular season and barely a thread of hope alive for a playoff spot, Matz's potion finally ran out, as he gave up six runs to the hapless Jeters. Two days later, the Mets were eliminated from postseason contention. Still, he managed to stay healthy enough to make 30 starts for the second season in a row, which was a major accomplishment for the lefty, even if his shocking transformations on the road were difficult to watch.

YEAR	TEAM	LVL	AGE	WHIP	ERA	DRA	WARP	MPH	FB%	WHF	CSP
2017	LVG	AAA	26	1.12	6.75	2.73	0.4				
2017	NYN	MLB	26	1.53	6.07	6.03	-0.3	94.8	59.1	7.9	48.4
2018	NYN	MLB	27	1.25	3.97	3.62	3.0	95.5	60	10	52.6
2019	NYN	MLB	28	1.34	4.21	4.39	2.4	95.1	50.7	10.6	50.5
2020	NYN	MLB	29	1.25	4.07	4.34	1.8	94.5	55.3	10	50.7

Steven Matz, continued

Pitch Shape vs LHH

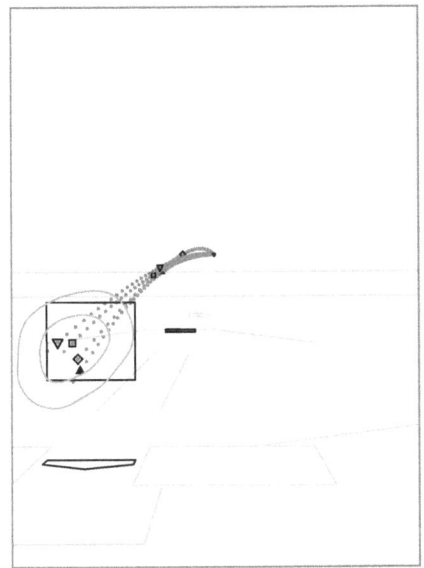

Pitch Shape vs RHH

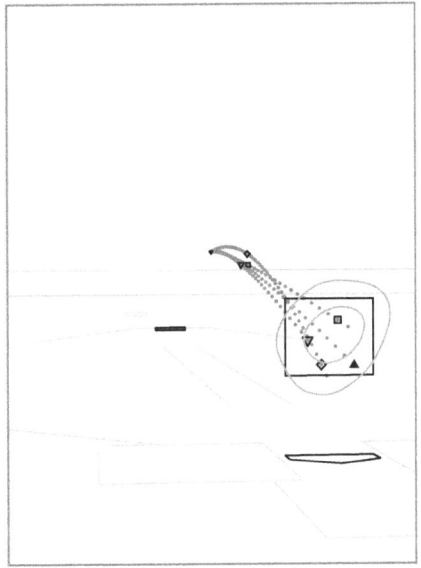

Type	Frequency	Velocity	H Movement	V Movement
● Fastball				
☐ Sinker	50.6%	93.6 [105]	14.4 [89]	-18.5 [107]
+ Cutter				
▲ Changeup	20.1%	84.5 [97]	15.3 [81]	-32.1 [86]
✕ Splitter				
▽ Slider	14.4%	89.7 [123]	2.9 [67]	-25.7 [121]
◇ Curveball	14.8%	78.7 [100]	-10.4 [112]	-46.8 [102]
⊕ Slow Curveball				
✻ Knuckleball				
▼ Screwball				

Rick Porcello RHP

Born: 12/27/88 Age: 31 Bats: R Throws: R
Height: 6'5" Weight: 205 Origin: Round 1, 2007 Draft (#27 overall)

YEAR	TEAM	LVL	AGE	W	L	SV	G	GS	IP	H	HR	BB/9	K/9	K	GB%	BABIP
2017	BOS	MLB	28	11	17	0	33	33	203¹	236	38	2.1	8.0	181	40%	.322
2018	BOS	MLB	29	17	7	0	33	33	191¹	177	27	2.3	8.9	190	45%	.285
2019	BOS	MLB	30	14	12	0	32	32	174¹	198	31	2.3	7.4	143	39%	.308
2020	NYN	MLB	31	7	7	0	21	21	107	112	21	2.4	7.4	88	39%	.289

Comparables: Rick Wise, Mike Witt, Alex Fernandez

In *A Storm of Swords*, Ser Barristan Selmy tells Daenerys Targaryen, "Every time a Targaryen is born, the gods toss a coin in the air and the world holds its breath to see how it will land." Well, every time Porcello started a season, the Red Sox were left in a similar state of respiratory suspense. The Sox didn't win the coin toss in 2019, as Porcello not only had the worst showing of his turbulent stint in Boston, but of his entire career. Porcello was a bottom-25 starter by DRA and a bottom-20 starter by ERA. He finished 11th in the majors in home runs allowed. In a stark reversal of his recent trends, he threw his slider less and his sinker more as the season went on, but to no avail. Maybe the new baseballs killed Porcello, but it's tough to give the benefit of the doubt to a player who rises and falls like bitcoin value. Porcello ended his Red Sox tenure having won a Cy Young and a World Series, but also having provided two truly terrible years and a third so-so one in the middle. He's too young, too durable and too talented not to rebound, but come April a new fanbase in Queens will be the ones holding their breath.

YEAR	TEAM	LVL	AGE	WHIP	ERA	DRA	WARP	MPH	FB%	WHF	CSP
2017	BOS	MLB	28	1.40	4.65	4.84	1.7	94.3	59.4	10.4	49.1
2018	BOS	MLB	29	1.18	4.28	4.02	2.8	93.2	50	9.6	48.9
2019	BOS	MLB	30	1.39	5.52	6.06	-0.5	92.8	56.5	8.9	49.1
2020	NYN	MLB	31	1.31	4.73	4.98	1.0	92.5	54.8	9.5	48.7

Rick Porcello, continued

Pitch Shape vs LHH

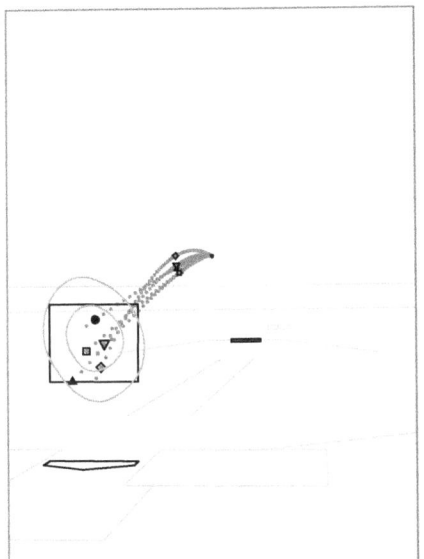

Pitch Shape vs RHH

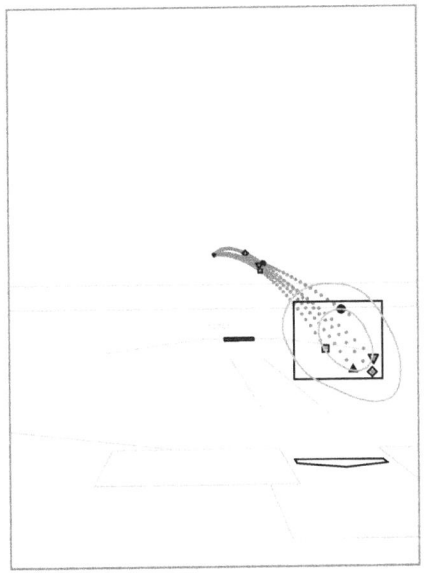

Type	Frequency	Velocity	H Movement	V Movement
● Fastball	31.6%	91.3 [97]	-7.9 [95]	-15.8 [100]
□ Sinker	24.8%	89.9 [86]	-14.6 [87]	-23.6 [89]
+ Cutter				
▲ Changeup	12.3%	81.3 [86]	-12.4 [94]	-30.6 [91]
✕ Splitter				
▽ Slider	18.6%	84.5 [101]	3.1 [92]	-30.3 [108]
◇ Curveball	12.6%	75 [88]	13.1 [123]	-50.2 [95]
⊕ Slow Curveball				
✻ Knuckleball				
▼ Screwball				

Mets Player Analysis - 65

Jacob Rhame RHP

Born: 03/16/93 Age: 27 Bats: R Throws: R
Height: 6'1" Weight: 215 Origin: Round 6, 2013 Draft (#184 overall)

YEAR	TEAM	LVL	AGE	W	L	SV	G	GS	IP	H	HR	BB/9	K/9	K	GB%	BABIP
2017	OKL	AAA	24	0	2	2	41	0	48	52	6	1.9	10.3	55	34%	.351
2017	LVG	AAA	24	0	1	0	4	0	6	2	0	0.0	16.5	11	44%	.222
2017	NYN	MLB	24	1	1	0	9	0	9	12	2	7.0	7.0	7	39%	.345
2018	LVG	AAA	25	1	2	11	25	0	32^1	22	4	2.2	11.4	41	32%	.250
2018	NYN	MLB	25	1	2	1	30	0	32^1	38	8	2.2	7.8	28	30%	.316
2019	SYR	AAA	26	3	2	3	20	0	19^2	19	4	2.7	11.4	25	35%	.312
2019	NYN	MLB	26	0	1	0	5	0	6^1	3	1	12.8	7.1	5	38%	.133
2020	NYN	MLB	27	1	1	0	25	0	27	24	6	3.3	8.7	26	32%	.258

Comparables: Nick Rumbelow, Heath Hembree, Silvino Bracho

Rhame's reign of terror ended in August after he underwent ulnar nerve surgery. He gained notoriety earlier in the season when he threw near the head of Rhys Hoskins, leading to an inevitable home run and a trot that was slower than Bartolo Colón's. Rhame routinely had control issues so it was legitimately possible he did not mean to throw near the slugger's head. Still he was suspended, sent to the minors and appeared in only two more games at the major-league level before undergoing surgery. All-in-all, a very Metsian year for the reliever.

YEAR	TEAM	LVL	AGE	WHIP	ERA	DRA	WARP	MPH	FB%	WHF	CSP
2017	OKL	AAA	24	1.29	4.31	3.65	0.9				
2017	LVG	AAA	24	0.33	1.50	5.82	0.0				
2017	NYN	MLB	24	2.11	9.00	7.37	-0.2	96.9	61.6	11.9	49.5
2018	LVG	AAA	25	0.93	3.06	2.19	1.1				
2018	NYN	MLB	25	1.42	5.85	4.84	0.0	97.8	68.5	15.2	50.9
2019	SYR	AAA	26	1.27	5.49	4.15	0.4				
2019	NYN	MLB	26	1.89	4.26	6.95	-0.1	97.5	67.8	8.3	45.2
2020	NYN	MLB	27	1.27	4.41	4.70	0.2	97.1	68	13.5	48.7

Jacob Rhame, continued

Pitch Shape vs LHH   Pitch Shape vs RHH

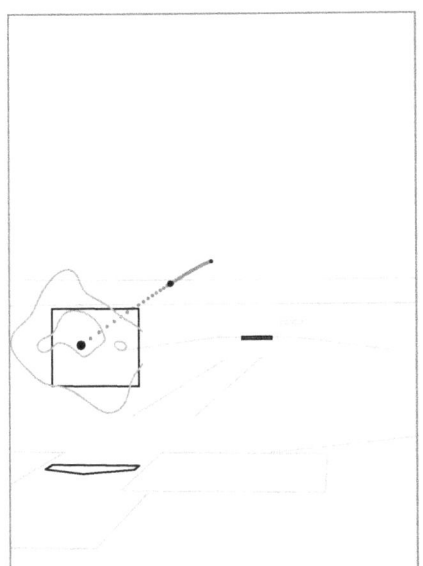 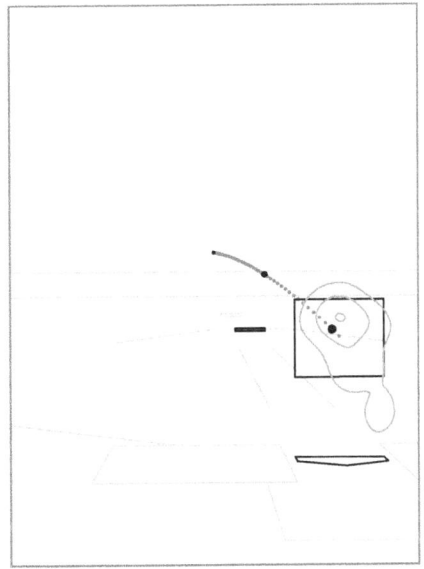

Type	Frequency	Velocity	H Movement	V Movement
● Fastball	67.8%	95.2 [108]	-9.9 [86]	-11.7 [111]
☐ Sinker				
+ Cutter				
▲ Changeup	22.3%	85.6 [101]	-14.6 [84]	-23.1 [113]
✕ Splitter				
▽ Slider	9.9%	87 [111]	4.5 [98]	-29.4 [111]
◇ Curveball				
⊕ Slow Curveball				
✳ Knuckleball				
▼ Screwball				

Paul Sewald RHP

Born: 05/26/90 Age: 30 Bats: R Throws: R
Height: 6'3" Weight: 207 Origin: Round 10, 2012 Draft (#320 overall)

YEAR	TEAM	LVL	AGE	W	L	SV	G	GS	IP	H	HR	BB/9	K/9	K	GB%	BABIP
2017	LVG	AAA	27	1	0	4	8	0	8^2	7	1	2.1	12.5	12	27%	.286
2017	NYN	MLB	27	0	6	0	57	0	65^1	58	8	2.9	9.5	69	35%	.287
2018	LVG	AAA	28	3	0	1	7	0	8	7	0	1.1	7.9	7	62%	.292
2018	NYN	MLB	28	0	7	2	46	0	56^1	62	8	3.7	9.3	58	32%	.331
2019	SYR	AAA	29	3	3	3	41	0	51	56	6	2.6	9.2	52	40%	.357
2019	NYN	MLB	29	1	1	1	17	0	19^2	18	3	1.4	10.1	22	17%	.294
2020	NYN	MLB	30	1	1	0	15	0	16	14	3	2.4	8.2	15	32%	.258

Comparables: Emilio Pagán, Richard Rodríguez, Josh Lueke

At one point during The LEGO Movie, one of Lord Business' robot minions says Emmet's face "is so generic it matches every other face in our database." That was Sewald in the Mets bullpen. Aside from the fact that he looks like a plain-faced LEGO man, nothing about Sewald or his stuff distinguished him from a bevy of Quad-A relievers in the Mets system. This was Sewald's third year in the league and he has tried everything from changing arm angles to the Tom Brady diet, which seemed to work for a bit but it evaporated faster than a 28-3 lead. At this point, if Sewald is in the game you know everything is not awesome.

YEAR	TEAM	LVL	AGE	WHIP	ERA	DRA	WARP	MPH	FB%	WHF	CSP
2017	LVG	AAA	27	1.04	2.08	2.14	0.3				
2017	NYN	MLB	27	1.21	4.55	3.59	1.2	93.6	64	12.3	50.4
2018	LVG	AAA	28	1.00	1.12	2.87	0.2				
2018	NYN	MLB	28	1.51	6.07	4.24	0.4	92.6	63.4	10.3	50.6
2019	SYR	AAA	29	1.39	3.35	4.02	1.1				
2019	NYN	MLB	29	1.07	4.58	5.31	0.0	93.6	70.6	10	55.4
2020	NYN	MLB	30	1.17	4.04	4.39	0.2	92.4	64.7	11	52.4

Paul Sewald, continued

Pitch Shape vs LHH

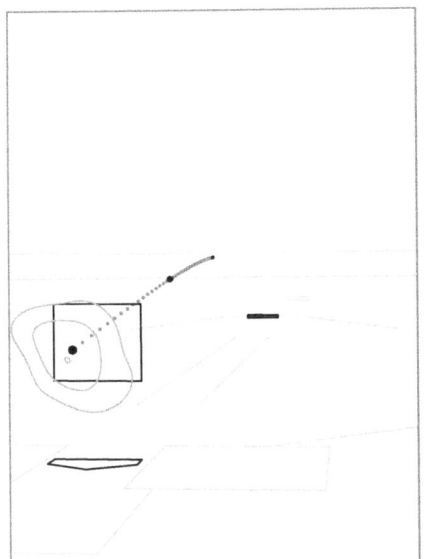

Pitch Shape vs RHH

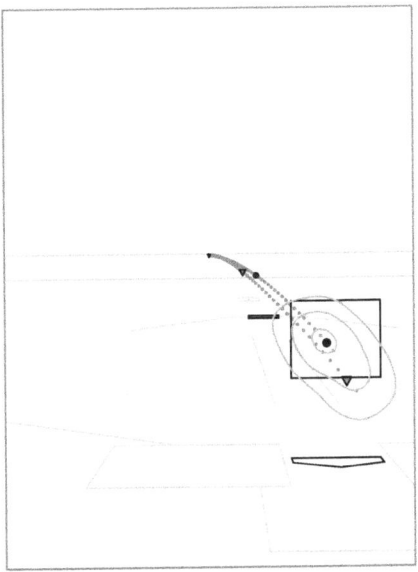

Type	Frequency	Velocity	H Movement	V Movement
● Fastball	69.7%	91.3 [97]	-10 [86]	-16.9 [97]
☐ Sinker				
+ Cutter				
▲ Changeup	3.6%	81.4 [86]	-12.8 [93]	-33.4 [82]
✕ Splitter				
▽ Slider	25.8%	82 [90]	10.4 [123]	-32.4 [102]
◇ Curveball				
⬥ Slow Curveball				
✳ Knuckleball				
▼ Screwball				

Marcus Stroman RHP

Born: 05/01/91   Age: 29   Bats: R   Throws: R
Height: 5'7"   Weight: 180   Origin: Round 1, 2012 Draft (#22 overall)

YEAR	TEAM	LVL	AGE	W	L	SV	G	GS	IP	H	HR	BB/9	K/9	K	GB%	BABIP
2017	TOR	MLB	26	13	9	0	33	33	201	201	21	2.8	7.3	164	63%	.310
2018	TOR	MLB	27	4	9	0	19	19	102^1	115	9	3.2	6.8	77	64%	.326
2019	TOR	MLB	28	6	11	0	21	21	124^2	118	10	2.5	7.1	99	56%	.293
2019	NYN	MLB	28	4	2	0	11	11	59^2	65	8	3.5	9.1	60	49%	.337
2020	NYN	MLB	29	10	9	0	28	28	162	162	21	3.0	7.7	140	55%	.298

Comparables: Kevin Gausman, Sonny Gray, Alex Cobb

Stroman didn't get traded to the New York team he expected when the Mets made a stunning move at the deadline, but he was a quality addition to the rotation in Queens. The Mets won his first four starts, helping to draw them back into an ultimately unsuccessful playoff chase, and were 8-3 overall when he toed the rubber. He even threw in seven scoreless innings at Coors Field for good measure. His charm and personality drew fans in from the get-go, especially compared with his more reserved rotation-mates, and a slightly more fastball-heavy approach once he got to Queens elevated both his strikeout and home-run rates—an extremely 2019 thing to do. With one more year left until free agency, Stroman will line up as the Mets' third starter in 2020 and his extended run of above-average performance will help solidify an already strong rotation.

YEAR	TEAM	LVL	AGE	WHIP	ERA	DRA	WARP	MPH	FB%	WHF	CSP
2017	TOR	MLB	26	1.31	3.09	4.18	3.1	95.2	62.2	10.6	46.7
2018	TOR	MLB	27	1.48	5.54	4.19	1.3	93.9	49.3	9.8	47.3
2019	TOR	MLB	28	1.23	2.96	3.74	2.8	94.1	44.1	10.8	45.1
2019	NYN	MLB	28	1.47	3.77	3.91	1.2	93.3	44.1	11.6	43.6
2020	NYN	MLB	29	1.34	4.09	4.31	2.7	93.6	50.6	10.7	46

Marcus Stroman, continued

Pitch Shape vs LHH

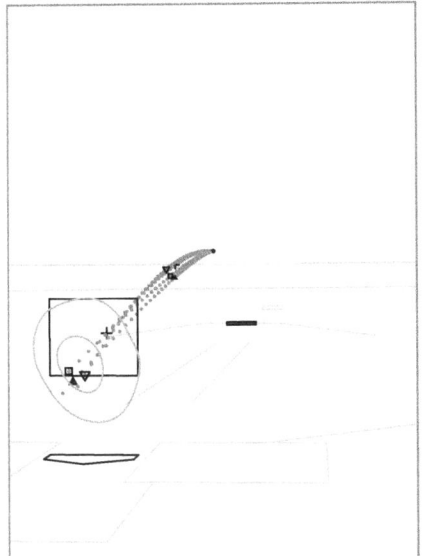

Pitch Shape vs RHH

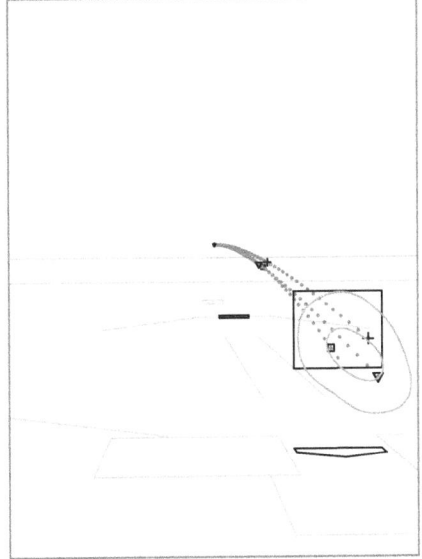

Type	Frequency	Velocity	H Movement	V Movement
● Fastball				
□ Sinker	37.5%	92.7 [100]	-10.3 [115]	-24.3 [86]
+ Cutter	24.6%	91.2 [116]	1.2 [96]	-23.3 [103]
▲ Changeup	4.5%	86.9 [106]	-12 [96]	-26 [104]
× Splitter				
▽ Slider	30.6%	85.9 [106]	9.8 [120]	-32.4 [102]
◇ Curveball				
⊕ Slow Curveball				
✳ Knuckleball				
▼ Screwball				

Noah Syndergaard RHP
Born: 08/29/92 Age: 27 Bats: L Throws: R
Height: 6'6" Weight: 240 Origin: Round 1, 2010 Draft (#38 overall)

YEAR	TEAM	LVL	AGE	W	L	SV	G	GS	IP	H	HR	BB/9	K/9	K	GB%	BABIP
2017	NYN	MLB	24	1	2	0	7	7	30[1]	29	0	0.9	10.1	34	59%	.337
2018	NYN	MLB	25	13	4	0	25	25	154[1]	148	9	2.3	9.0	155	50%	.320
2019	NYN	MLB	26	10	8	0	32	32	197[2]	194	24	2.3	9.2	202	48%	.313
2020	NYN	MLB	27	12	8	0	28	28	168	148	18	2.4	9.5	178	48%	.293

Comparables: Carlos Martínez, Aaron Nola, Gerrit Cole

A desolate, abandoned Citi Field was the result of *spoiler alert* Thanos turning half of humanity into ash. Thor made a valiant attempt to avoid the disaster but it was too late. The god of thunder spiraled pretty quickly from his mistake and wasn't the same hero everyone came to expect. Life imitated art a little too closely when Syndergaard struggled on the top-line in 2019, having the worst season of his MLB career and leading the league in earned runs allowed. Despite that, Thor still finished had a top-20 DRA among the 69 pitchers who threw at least 150 innings last season—further highlighting that "worst" is awfully relative. More troubling was that he backed off his devastating slider that early in the year he had zero confidence in and throughout the year carried diminished velocity. With a new manager and new pitching coach in town for 2020, Syndergaard will look to regain his elite form, and rediscovering his best offspeed pitch is tantamount. In fact, a hard turn into a pitch mix that features it more often at the expense of his fastball would help avenge his trend of diminishing strikeouts.

YEAR	TEAM	LVL	AGE	WHIP	ERA	DRA	WARP	MPH	FB%	WHF	CSP
2017	NYN	MLB	24	1.05	2.97	2.54	1.0	100.6	51.3	14.9	47
2018	NYN	MLB	25	1.21	3.03	2.47	5.0	99.9	53.7	14.4	47.5
2019	NYN	MLB	26	1.23	4.28	3.40	5.1	99.6	59.2	13.7	50.1
2020	NYN	MLB	27	1.14	3.07	3.41	4.5	99.3	57.5	14.2	49

Noah Syndergaard, continued

Pitch Shape vs LHH

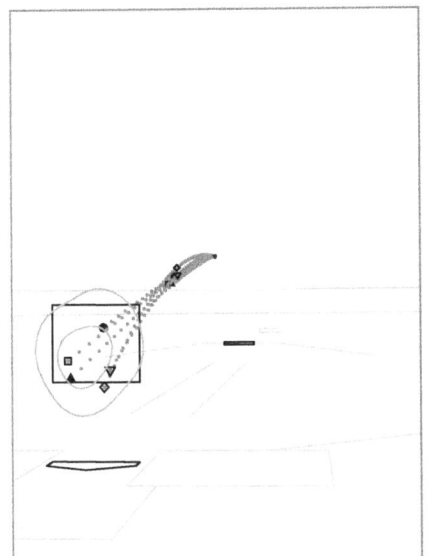

Pitch Shape vs RHH

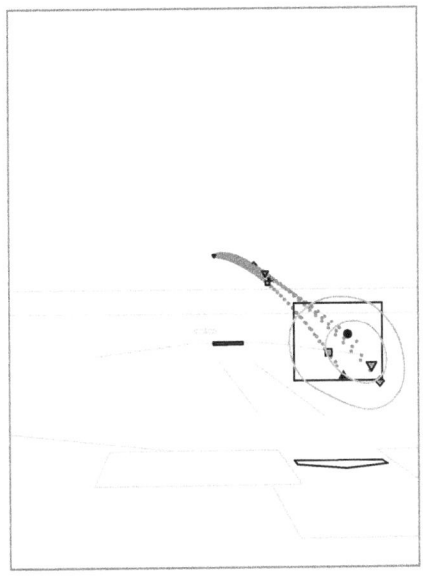

Type	Frequency	Velocity	H Movement	V Movement
● Fastball	29.3%	98.1 [116]	-5.1 [108]	-12.4 [109]
☐ Sinker	29.9%	97.9 [128]	-12.4 [102]	-17.1 [112]
+ Cutter				
▲ Changeup	16.1%	91.5 [123]	-13.6 [89]	-22.1 [116]
✕ Splitter				
▽ Slider	15.2%	89.4 [121]	3.6 [94]	-30 [109]
◇ Curveball	9.5%	80.7 [107]	11 [114]	-40.5 [115]
⊕ Slow Curveball				
✳ Knuckleball				
▼ Screwball				

Michael Wacha RHP

Born: 07/01/91   Age: 28   Bats: R   Throws: R
Height: 6'6"   Weight: 215   Origin: Round 1, 2012 Draft (#19 overall)

YEAR	TEAM	LVL	AGE	W	L	SV	G	GS	IP	H	HR	BB/9	K/9	K	GB%	BABIP
2017	SLN	MLB	25	12	9	0	30	30	165²	170	17	3.0	8.6	158	50%	.327
2018	SLN	MLB	26	8	2	0	15	15	84¹	68	9	3.8	7.6	71	47%	.249
2019	SLN	MLB	27	6	7	0	29	24	126²	143	26	3.9	7.4	104	50%	.313
2020	NYN	MLB	28	6	6	0	33	18	103	102	15	3.4	7.5	86	47%	.288

Comparables: Julio Teheran, Shelby Miller, Mat Latos

Wacha might never recapture his transcendent 2013 form, but you have to admit: 2019 felt like a logical end to a riches-to-rags story arc. After years of bouncing between good and hurt, the cumulative toll of injuries caught up to him; not only has his fastball has never been slower than it was in 2019, it's never featured less rise, either. Wacha has always leaned heavily on his fastball and changeup, and losing one of those two pillars of his game was simply too much to withstand. He looked a bit better in the second half of the season in two-to-four-inning spurts, and that ought to be his role going forward. That his fastball didn't seem to perk up in shorter outings could be a sign that he's just not going to find sustainable success again.

YEAR	TEAM	LVL	AGE	WHIP	ERA	DRA	WARP	MPH	FB%	WHF	CSP
2017	SLN	MLB	25	1.36	4.13	3.83	3.2	97.5	52.8	10.9	49.9
2018	SLN	MLB	26	1.23	3.20	3.98	1.3	96.3	43.1	10.4	46.2
2019	SLN	MLB	27	1.56	4.76	6.25	-0.7	95.5	50.8	10.1	46.3
2020	NYN	MLB	28	1.36	4.37	4.56	1.4	95.8	50	10.5	47.5

Michael Wacha, continued

Pitch Shape vs LHH

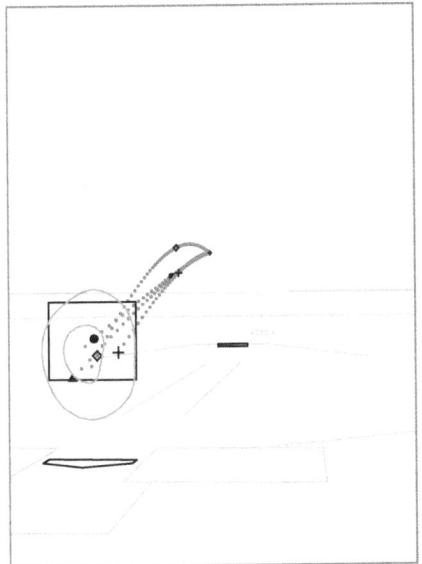

Pitch Shape vs RHH

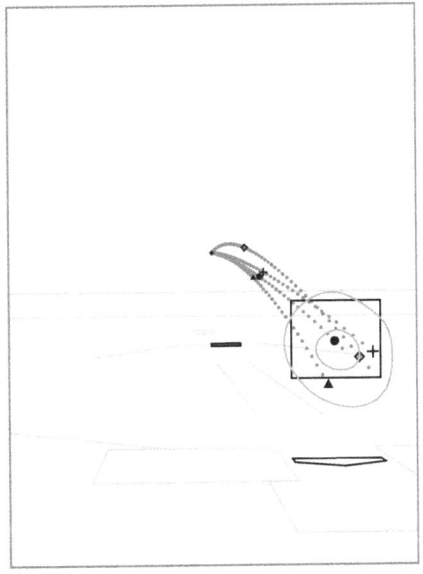

Type	Frequency	Velocity	H Movement	V Movement
● Fastball	49.5%	93.4 [103]	-5.8 [105]	-12.8 [108]
☐ Sinker				
+ Cutter	15.1%	89.7 [107]	2.1 [101]	-20.4 [113]
▲ Changeup	23.8%	85.9 [102]	-9.8 [106]	-24.9 [107]
✕ Splitter				
▽ Slider				
◇ Curveball	10.3%	75.6 [90]	7.9 [102]	-52.9 [89]
⊕ Slow Curveball				
✳ Knuckleball				
▼ Screwball				

Justin Wilson   LHP

Born: 08/18/87   Age: 32   Bats: L   Throws: L
Height: 6'2"   Weight: 205   Origin: Round 5, 2008 Draft (#144 overall)

YEAR	TEAM	LVL	AGE	W	L	SV	G	GS	IP	H	HR	BB/9	K/9	K	GB%	BABIP
2017	DET	MLB	29	3	4	13	42	0	40^1	22	5	3.6	12.3	55	38%	.210
2017	CHN	MLB	29	1	0	0	23	0	17^2	18	0	9.7	12.7	25	37%	.391
2018	CHN	MLB	30	4	5	0	71	0	54^2	45	5	5.4	11.4	69	37%	.310
2019	NYN	MLB	31	4	2	4	45	0	39	33	4	4.4	10.2	44	52%	.299
2020	NYN	MLB	32	2	2	0	45	0	48	39	6	4.0	9.7	52	44%	.271

Comparables: Jeremy Jeffress, Brian Wilson, Randy Myers

Despite being injured for a good chunk of the year, Wilson's signing was one of Brodie Van Wagenen's best moves of last offseason. That statement sounds like an indictment, but in this case it's not. Wilson's elbow inflammation helped to descend the bullpen into chaos, but they relied on that appendage heavily in the second half of the season. In fact, between the start of the All-Star Break and when Wilson was shut down after the Mets were eliminated from the playoffs, the southpaw pitched in 52 percent of the team's games—a higher rate than Alex Claudio, who led baseball in appearances. Wilson was even tasked with closing four games out in September when the bullpen was in full-on committee mode and his lack of a platoon split—thanks to a cutter than holds righties in check—made him a valuable late-inning weapon. If his elbow holds up after such heavy use, he'll assume the same bullpen role in 2020.

YEAR	TEAM	LVL	AGE	WHIP	ERA	DRA	WARP	MPH	FB%	WHF	CSP
2017	DET	MLB	29	0.94	2.68	3.24	0.9	97.8	64.3	16	49.2
2017	CHN	MLB	29	2.09	5.09	6.03	-0.2	97.2	64.3	9.2	46.5
2018	CHN	MLB	30	1.43	3.46	4.65	0.2	96.3	75.4	13.4	51.9
2019	NYN	MLB	31	1.33	2.54	3.51	0.8	96.5	52.4	12.6	49
2020	NYN	MLB	32	1.26	3.46	3.71	0.9	95.8	64.1	13	49.3

Justin Wilson, continued

Pitch Shape vs LHH

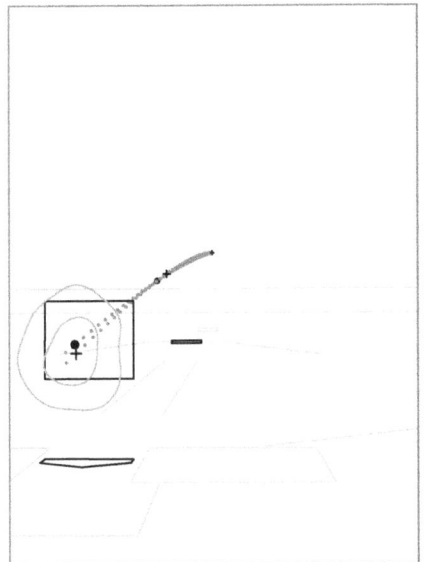

Pitch Shape vs RHH

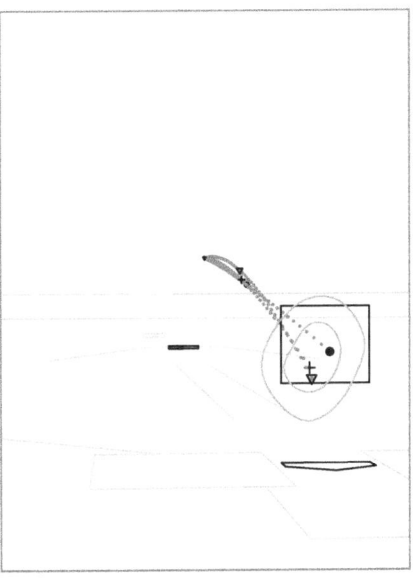

Type	Frequency	Velocity	H Movement	V Movement
● Fastball	52.4%	95.2 [108]	3.7 [114]	-10.6 [114]
☐ Sinker				
+ Cutter	39.2%	90.3 [110]	-4.2 [114]	-21.9 [108]
▲ Changeup				
✕ Splitter				
▽ Slider	8.4%	84.1 [99]	-5.6 [102]	-36.8 [89]
◇ Curveball				
✦ Slow Curveball				
✳ Knuckleball				
▼ Screwball				

Mets Player Analysis - 77

Jacob deGrom RHP

Born: 06/19/88 Age: 32 Bats: L Throws: R
Height: 6'4" Weight: 180 Origin: Round 9, 2010 Draft (#272 overall)

YEAR	TEAM	LVL	AGE	W	L	SV	G	GS	IP	H	HR	BB/9	K/9	K	GB%	BABIP
2017	NYN	MLB	29	15	10	0	31	31	201[1]	180	28	2.6	10.7	239	48%	.305
2018	NYN	MLB	30	10	9	0	32	32	217	152	10	1.9	11.2	269	48%	.281
2019	NYN	MLB	31	11	8	0	32	32	204	154	19	1.9	11.2	255	45%	.282
2020	NYN	MLB	32	13	8	0	29	29	187	145	21	2.4	11.3	235	45%	.285

Comparables: Corey Kluber, Collin McHugh, Mike Bolsinger

The combination of David Wright's influence as a new front office member, Noah Syndergaard's public plea and 7-Eleven taquitos helped deGrom sign a contract extension, fresh off a Cy Young-winning season. Regression was expected after the cheat code numbers deGrom put up in 2018, but he was almost the exact same pitcher on the whole. After the All-Star Break, deGrom pitched to a 1.44 ERA and a 0.83 WHIP after ramping up the usage of his devastating slider to great effect. His signature consistency, combined with an uptick in velocity on his entire arsenal, left many batters walking away from the box shaking their heads in disbelief. Ultimately, the right-hander became the first pitcher in franchise history to bring home the Cy Young hardware in consecutive seasons—although that's only because Dwight Gooden was completely hosed in 1984.

YEAR	TEAM	LVL	AGE	WHIP	ERA	DRA	WARP	MPH	FB%	WHF	CSP
2017	NYN	MLB	29	1.19	3.53	3.02	5.7	97.7	55.5	14.5	49.5
2018	NYN	MLB	30	0.91	1.70	2.09	8.0	98.5	52.1	16.3	48.4
2019	NYN	MLB	31	0.97	2.43	2.27	7.8	98.9	49.3	16.9	46.5
2020	NYN	MLB	32	1.05	2.52	2.90	6.0	97.5	51.3	16	47.5

Jacob deGrom, continued

Pitch Shape vs LHH

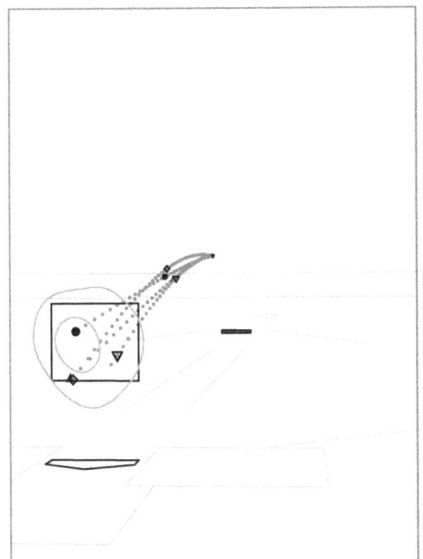

Pitch Shape vs RHH

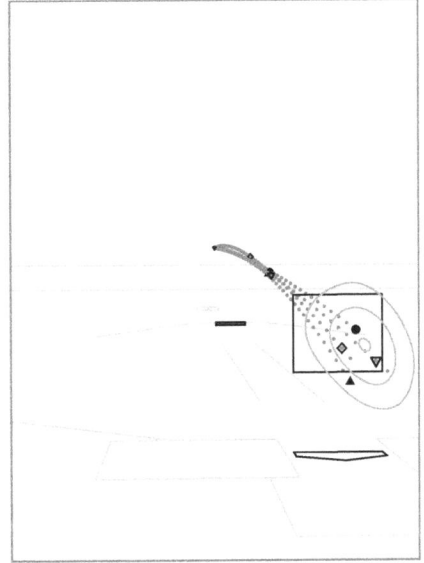

Type	Frequency	Velocity	H Movement	V Movement
● Fastball	48.8%	97.3 [114]	-4.8 [109]	-11.1 [113]
☐ Sinker				
+ Cutter				
▲ Changeup	15.9%	90.6 [119]	-12 [96]	-26.1 [104]
✕ Splitter				
▽ Slider	31.9%	92.8 [135]	3.2 [92]	-22.1 [132]
◇ Curveball				
✦ Slow Curveball				
✱ Knuckleball				
▼ Screwball				

PLAYER COMMENTS WITHOUT GRAPHS

Francisco Alvarez C
Born: 11/19/01   Age: 18   Bats: R   Throws: R
Height: 5'11"   Weight: 220   Origin: International Free Agent, 2018

YEAR	TEAM	LVL	AGE	PA	R	2B	3B	HR	RBI	BB	K	SB	CS	AVG/OBP/SLG
2019	MTS	RK	17	31	8	4	0	2	10	4	4	0	1	.462/.548/.846
2019	KNG	RK+	17	151	24	6	0	5	16	17	33	1	1	.282/.377/.443
2020	NYN	MLB	18	251	24	12	1	5	25	24	75	3	1	.231/.313/.356

Comparables: Oscar Hernández, Gary Sánchez, Jefry Marte

The Mets are a franchise whose catching situation has often been muddled ever since Mike Piazza left in 2005. Trying to rectify that, the team went all out and signed Alvarez out of Venezuela to a team record $2.9 million deal in 2018. To say the early returns have been promising for the teenager is an understatement as big as the teenager's arm. After obliterating complex-league pitchers so thoroughly that he was moved up to the Appy League after only 31 plate appearances, Alvarez was a well above-average hitter while being one of the youngest players in the league and getting his first experience catching pro pitchers. He remains a ways away from contributing in Queens, despite being advanced for his age. He's got work to do on his receiving behind the plate but getting the heightened attention of prospect hounds in your first stateside season is quite a feat.

YEAR	TEAM	LVL	AGE	PA	DRC+	VORP	BABIP	BRR	FRAA	WARP
2019	MTS	RK	17	31	224	7.7	.500	-0.3	C(4): 0.3	0.4
2019	KNG	RK+	17	151	128	9.1	.344	-1.4		0.9
2020	NYN	MLB	18	251	82	2.3	.325	0.0	C 0	0.2

Brett Baty 3B

Born: 11/13/99   Age: 20   Bats: L   Throws: R
Height: 6'3"   Weight: 210   Origin: Round 1, 2019 Draft (#12 overall)

YEAR	TEAM	LVL	AGE	PA	R	2B	3B	HR	RBI	BB	K	SB	CS	AVG/OBP/SLG
2019	MTS	RK	19	25	5	3	0	1	8	5	6	0	0	.350/.480/.650
2019	KNG	RK+	19	186	30	12	2	6	22	24	56	0	0	.222/.339/.437
2020	NYN	MLB	20	251	21	12	1	4	21	25	92	2	1	.186/.276/.300

Comparables: Carlos Peguero, Chris Carter, José Altuve

Baty was old for a high school draftee, which may have led some teams to shy away from him in the first round of the 2019 draft but the Mets went for the then 19-and-a-half-year-old with the twelfth overall pick. At the plate, he showcases easy plus raw power and shows a discerning approach that in time should develop a shade more aggressiveness when appropriate. On the field, the Texan looks the part of someone who can hold down the hot corner until his body starts to turn—it's just a matter of when that might be. But for an organization that just graduated the NL Rookie of the Year and a fanbase that is ready for the next next big thing, expectations are going to be an issue. In fact, when he was selected, Harold Reynolds described Baty on the MLB Network broadcast as "Freddie Freeman with power." Freeman only hit *checks notes* 38 home runs last season, so no pressure, kid.

YEAR	TEAM	LVL	AGE	PA	DRC+	VORP	BABIP	BRR	FRAA	WARP
2019	MTS	RK	19	25	148	4.1	.462	0.2	3B(4): -0.2	0.2
2019	KNG	RK+	19	186	108	5.5	.302	-0.4		0.6
2020	NYN	MLB	20	251	57	-5.9	.297	0.0	3B 0	-0.6

Yoenis Céspedes LF

Born: 10/18/85 Age: 34 Bats: R Throws: R
Height: 5'10" Weight: 220 Origin: International Free Agent, 2012

YEAR	TEAM	LVL	AGE	PA	R	2B	3B	HR	RBI	BB	K	SB	CS	AVG/OBP/SLG
2017	NYN	MLB	31	321	46	17	2	17	42	26	61	0	1	.292/.352/.540
2018	NYN	MLB	32	157	20	6	0	9	29	13	50	3	0	.262/.325/.496
2020	NYN	MLB	34	217	28	9	1	13	34	16	55	2	1	.249/.310/.493

Comparables: Willie Horton, Gene Oliver, Jeromy Burnitz

Nearly a decade after he burst onto the U.S. baseball scene with a workout video for the ages, La Potencia has captivated four different fanbases—well, maybe not the Red Sox—and flashed the talent that led Kevin Goldstein to call him the best all-around prospect to come out of Cuba in a generation. In New York, he's a legend both on the field and off, his hitting prowess from 2015 and 2016 nearly as memorable as his many spring training rides—both of the sports car and equine variety. Unfortunately, that fame has been stymied by unusual injuries that have conspired to limit him to 119 games over the last three years. This culminated with surgery to remove calcification on both heels in late 2018, followed by a severely broken ankle in May—quite possibly the only boar-related injury of the 2019 season. There's almost nothing Céspedes could do that would surprise anyone at this point, except possibly for returning as a middle-of-the-order thumper to lead the Mets in his final contract year.

YEAR	TEAM	LVL	AGE	PA	DRC+	VORP	BABIP	BRR	FRAA	WARP
2017	NYN	MLB	31	321	123	23.6	.316	-1.1	LF(74): 2.9	1.9
2018	NYN	MLB	32	157	99	11.3	.333	0.5	LF(35): 1.8	0.6
2020	NYN	MLB	34	217	111	8.7	.280	-0.2	LF 2	1.1

Andrés Giménez SS

Born: 09/04/98 Age: 21 Bats: L Throws: R
Height: 6'0" Weight: 161 Origin: International Free Agent, 2015

YEAR	TEAM	LVL	AGE	PA	R	2B	3B	HR	RBI	BB	K	SB	CS	AVG/OBP/SLG
2017	COL	A	18	399	50	9	4	4	31	28	61	14	8	.265/.346/.349
2018	SLU	A+	19	351	43	20	4	6	30	22	70	28	11	.282/.348/.432
2018	BIN	AA	19	153	19	9	1	0	16	9	22	10	3	.277/.344/.358
2019	BIN	AA	20	479	54	22	5	9	37	24	102	28	16	.250/.309/.387
2020	NYN	MLB	21	35	3	1	0	1	3	2	9	1	0	.229/.287/.357

Comparables: Rougned Odor, Jake Bauers, Francisco Lindor

It was a year of return engagements for the 21-year-old shortstop, first in Binghamton and then in the Arizona Fall League. Giménez was the Mets' consensus top prospect in the organization once Pete Alonso graduated to the majors, but sputtered after a change to his swing—designed to get him to leverage his strength better—didn't take hold. While he's been passed in those pesky org rankings, the base package of defense at the six and speed still remain and will propel him to a major-league future. The difference between that future being an everyday starting spot or a utility role will ultimately come down to his hit tool, which was still somewhat evident when he took home the 2019 batting title in the AFL. Giménez is still young enough to get back to track as long as he isn't too Metsed up.

YEAR	TEAM	LVL	AGE	PA	DRC+	VORP	BABIP	BRR	FRAA	WARP
2017	COL	A	18	399	110	22.3	.310	0.7	SS(89): 6.6	2.9
2018	SLU	A+	19	351	113	24.8	.343	3.4	SS(83): 14.2, 2B(2): -0.1	3.8
2018	BIN	AA	19	153	102	8.4	.330	1.2	SS(36): -1.3, 2B(1): 0.2	0.7
2019	BIN	AA	20	479	92	17.9	.306	-2.9	SS(111): -0.7	1.3
2020	NYN	MLB	21	35	71	0.0	.289	0.0	SS 0	0.0

Luis Guillorme SS

Born: 09/27/94 Age: 25 Bats: L Throws: R
Height: 5'10" Weight: 195 Origin: Round 10, 2013 Draft (#296 overall)

YEAR	TEAM	LVL	AGE	PA	R	2B	3B	HR	RBI	BB	K	SB	CS	AVG/OBP/SLG
2017	BIN	AA	22	558	70	20	0	1	43	72	55	4	3	.283/.376/.331
2018	LVG	AAA	23	281	41	15	2	3	33	30	39	2	1	.304/.380/.417
2018	NYN	MLB	23	74	4	2	0	0	5	7	3	1	0	.209/.284/.239
2019	SYR	AAA	24	278	33	12	0	7	32	39	42	4	4	.307/.412/.452
2019	NYN	MLB	24	70	8	4	0	1	3	7	14	0	0	.246/.324/.361
2020	NYN	MLB	25	147	14	6	0	2	13	15	26	1	0	.249/.328/.345

Comparables: Didi Gregorius, Tommy Brown, Johan Camargo

For an organization that successfully had Rey Ordoñez in its lineup for years, and for one that is currently significantly handicapped by its defense, one would think that Guillorme would get more of a look in the infield. Instead the organization steered into the skid, and he actually saw less action that the previous year despite putting up better numbers in Syracuse than he did in Las Vegas. *insert shrug emoji here*

YEAR	TEAM	LVL	AGE	PA	DRC+	VORP	BABIP	BRR	FRAA	WARP
2017	BIN	AA	22	558	116	25.2	.316	3.4	2B(72): 4.1, SS(58): -2.1	3.6
2018	LVG	AAA	23	281	107	12.3	.350	0.3	SS(54): 1.9, 2B(9): -1.4	1.7
2018	NYN	MLB	23	74	92	-0.5	.219	0.7	3B(14): -1.8, 2B(8): -0.5	0.0
2019	SYR	AAA	24	278	130	21.9	.346	0.7	2B(30): -0.3, SS(26): -0.9	1.9
2019	NYN	MLB	24	70	85	1.4	.304	0.4	SS(8): -0.2, 2B(8): 0.0	0.2
2020	NYN	MLB	25	147	85	1.4	.299	-0.3	SS 0, 3B -1	0.0

Jed Lowrie   INF

Born: 04/17/84   Age: 36   Bats: B   Throws: R
Height: 6'0"   Weight: 180   Origin: Round 1, 2005 Draft (#45 overall)

YEAR	TEAM	LVL	AGE	PA	R	2B	3B	HR	RBI	BB	K	SB	CS	AVG/OBP/SLG
2017	OAK	MLB	33	645	86	49	3	14	69	73	100	0	1	.277/.360/.448
2018	OAK	MLB	34	680	78	37	1	23	99	78	128	0	0	.267/.353/.448
2019	SYR	AAA	35	48	7	1	0	2	3	4	12	0	0	.250/.313/.409
2019	NYN	MLB	35	8	0	0	0	0	0	1	4	0	0	.000/.125/.000
2020	NYN	MLB	36	161	17	6	0	5	18	15	35	0	0	.231/.307/.384

Comparables: Eddie Bressoud, Roy Smalley, Tony Phillips

Eight plate appearances. Eight. After two straight full seasons in Oakland, Lowrie found the point of demarcation between injury prone and having Mr. Burns's Three Stooges syndrome. Calf, hamstring, left side, right side, head, shoulders, knees and toes; you name it, he tweaked it. To his credit he worked his way back and even helped the Brooklyn Cyclones in their quest for a championship along the way, which ironically made Lowrie the only active Met to appear in the playoffs last season. Counting on Lowrie to provide anything in 2020 aside from a $10 million hit to the Wilpons' self-imposed salary cap is a fool's errand, but here's hoping he can at least go back to his simply injury prone days.

YEAR	TEAM	LVL	AGE	PA	DRC+	VORP	BABIP	BRR	FRAA	WARP
2017	OAK	MLB	33	645	114	27.0	.314	-2.4	2B(136): -3.5, 3B(1): 0.2	2.4
2018	OAK	MLB	34	680	126	37.9	.304	-3.0	2B(136): -0.4, 3B(14): -0.5	3.9
2019	SYR	AAA	35	48	92	0.6	.300	0.5	2B(5): -0.5, 3B(5): -0.9	0.0
2019	NYN	MLB	35	8	71	-0.1	.000	0.1		0.0
2020	NYN	MLB	36	161	84	1.5	.271	-0.5	2B 0, 3B -1	0.0

Ronny Mauricio SS

Born: 04/04/01   Age: 19   Bats: B   Throws: R
Height: 6'3"   Weight: 166   Origin: International Free Agent, 2017

YEAR	TEAM	LVL	AGE	PA	R	2B	3B	HR	RBI	BB	K	SB	CS	AVG/OBP/SLG
2018	MTS	RK	17	212	26	13	3	3	31	10	31	1	6	.279/.307/.421
2018	KNG	RK	17	35	6	3	0	0	4	3	9	1	0	.233/.286/.333
2019	COL	A	18	504	62	20	5	4	37	23	99	6	10	.268/.307/.357
2020	NYN	MLB	19	251	22	12	1	3	22	20	66	1	1	.239/.302/.343

Comparables: Amed Rosario, Andrew Velazquez, Leury García

While Andrés Giménez left an opening to be surpassed as the team's top prospect, Mauricio's strong full-season debut and collection of tools made sure the door slammed loudly behind him. A potential plus hit tool drives the soon-to-be-19-year-old's profile and with some added strength on his frame and loft in his bat path, he should be able to push plus power in the future to match it. The switch hitter was stronger when swinging from the left side in 2019—though at this point in his development that's more about reps than anything else. With smooth motions and a strong arm, Mauricio could end up an above-average defender at either shortstop or third base. If that sounds a little like Carlos Correa, you're both naturally optimistic and not entirely wrong. It's a fun profile.

YEAR	TEAM	LVL	AGE	PA	DRC+	VORP	BABIP	BRR	FRAA	WARP
2018	MTS	RK	17	212	125	10.1	.310	-0.3	SS(45): 0.3	1.3
2018	KNG	RK	17	35	78	1.9	.304	0.5	SS(8): -0.1	0.1
2019	COL	A	18	504	100	24.4	.330	2.9	SS(106): -0.1	2.3
2020	NYN	MLB	19	251	74	-0.9	.321	-0.5	SS 1	0.0

Shervyen Newton INF

Born: 04/24/99 Age: 21 Bats: B Throws: R
Height: 6'4" Weight: 180 Origin: International Free Agent, 2015

YEAR	TEAM	LVL	AGE	PA	R	2B	3B	HR	RBI	BB	K	SB	CS	AVG/OBP/SLG
2017	MET	RK	18	303	51	11	9	1	31	50	57	10	4	.311/.433/.444
2018	KNG	RK	19	266	50	16	2	5	41	46	84	4	0	.280/.408/.449
2019	COL	A	20	423	35	15	2	9	32	37	139	1	4	.209/.283/.330
2020	NYN	MLB	21	251	22	11	1	5	23	23	96	0	0	.203/.282/.327

Comparables: Luis Rengifo, Drew Robinson, Teoscar Hernández

At every level of the organization, the Mets' cup seemingly runneth over at the shortstop position. In addition to Andrés Giménez and Ronny Mauricio, Newton is a worthy inclusion in the intriguing prospects category—though he bounced mostly between second and third last season in deference to Mauricio. A tall, switch-hitter, Newton has serious power potential that can bend the laws of physics, especially as he continues to grow. But for every action there is an equal and opposite reaction, and for how much pop is in his bat, the physics of a pitched ball can be equally confounding to the youngster.

YEAR	TEAM	LVL	AGE	PA	DRC+	VORP	BABIP	BRR	FRAA	WARP
2017	MET	RK	18	303	161	33.0	.398	-2.0	SS(60): 7.7, 3B(5): 0.8	3.7
2018	KNG	RK	19	266	124	24.5	.421	2.2	SS(49): 10.8, 2B(3): 0.3	3.0
2019	COL	A	20	423	86	3.9	.303	-2.0	2B(53): -0.4, SS(27): -2.0	0.2
2020	NYN	MLB	21	251	64	-4.2	.330	-0.4	SS 1, 2B 0	-0.3

Matthew Allan RHP

Born: 04/17/01 Age: 19 Bats: R Throws: R
Height: 6'3" Weight: 225 Origin: Round 3, 2019 Draft (#89 overall)

YEAR	TEAM	LVL	AGE	W	L	SV	G	GS	IP	H	HR	BB/9	K/9	K	GB%	BABIP
2019	MTS	RK	18	1	0	0	5	4	8^1	5	0	4.3	11.9	11	32%	.263
2020	NYN	MLB	19	2	2	0	33	0	35	35	5	3.8	8.2	32	41%	.296

Comparables: Jake Thompson, Tyler Glasnow, Neftalí Feliz

If there was any team in the league who would draft a prized arm and then not be able to sign him it would be the Mets. Especially since they had a rookie GM in his first draft with a revamped front office. While other teams shied away from Allan's asking price, it seemed the Mets got a steal when they drafted Allan 89th overall, especially since he was regarded as one of the best prep pitchers in the class. After drafting inexpensive college seniors in the following rounds, the Mets not only managed to avoid egg on their face by signing Allan, but inked him for a less-than-expected $2.5 million signing bonus. With a mid-90's fastball, a curve that flashes easy plus and the makings of a solid change, Allan immediately became the best pitching prospect in the system.

YEAR	TEAM	LVL	AGE	WHIP	ERA	DRA	WARP	MPH	FB%	WHF	CSP
2019	MTS	RK	18	1.08	1.08	2.36	0.3				
2020	NYN	MLB	19	1.42	4.74	4.82	0.2				

Dellin Betances   RHP

Born: 03/23/88   Age: 32   Bats: R   Throws: R
Height: 6'8"   Weight: 265   Origin: Round 8, 2006 Draft (#254 overall)

YEAR	TEAM	LVL	AGE	W	L	SV	G	GS	IP	H	HR	BB/9	K/9	K	GB%	BABIP
2017	NYA	MLB	29	3	6	10	66	0	59^2	29	3	6.6	15.1	100	49%	.252
2018	NYA	MLB	30	4	6	4	66	0	66^2	44	7	3.5	15.5	115	46%	.311
2019	NYA	MLB	31	0	0	0	1	0	0^2	0	0	0.0	27.0	2	0%	.000
2020	NYN	MLB	32	3	2	7	50	0	53	32	5	2.9	12.2	72	46%	.245

Comparables: Craig Kimbrel, Aroldis Chapman, Kenley Jansen

Despite a record-breaking number of injuries during the Yankees' 2019 season, Brian Cashman called Betances' "the most heart-breaking of the year." The big righty's frustration was palpable as he went through countless setbacks while trying to get back in fighting shape, struggling through a shoulder impingement before being slowed by a lat strain. But finally, on September 15, Betances toed the rubber in Toronto and struck out the first two batters he faced—for a second, all of the hard work in a lost season was going to pay off and he'd reprise a key role for a playoff-bound squad. Instead, he partially tore his Achilles and is now questionable for the start of the 2020 season. He managed two strikeouts in his lone appearance. Fate can be so cruel.

YEAR	TEAM	LVL	AGE	WHIP	ERA	DRA	WARP	MPH	FB%	WHF	CSP
2017	NYA	MLB	29	1.22	2.87	3.04	1.4	100.3	46.2	13.3	44.1
2018	NYA	MLB	30	1.05	2.70	2.15	2.1	99.9	47.8	16	47.1
2019	NYA	MLB	31	0.00	0.00	10.17	0.0	95.4	62.5	0	56
2020	NYN	MLB	32	0.92	1.60	2.38	1.8	99.0	46.8	14.7	49.6

Corey Oswalt RHP

Born: 09/03/93   Age: 26   Bats: R   Throws: R
Height: 6'5"   Weight: 250   Origin: Round 7, 2012 Draft (#230 overall)

YEAR	TEAM	LVL	AGE	W	L	SV	G	GS	IP	H	HR	BB/9	K/9	K	GB%	BABIP
2017	BIN	AA	23	12	5	0	24	24	134[1]	118	9	2.7	8.0	119	49%	.290
2018	LVG	AAA	24	4	4	0	11	11	52[1]	58	9	3.4	8.9	52	45%	.331
2018	NYN	MLB	24	3	3	0	17	12	64[2]	69	14	2.8	6.3	45	43%	.276
2019	BRO	A-	25	0	0	0	2	2	6	6	0	4.5	10.5	7	28%	.333
2019	SYR	AAA	25	10	4	0	16	16	86[2]	84	9	1.6	8.2	79	45%	.304
2019	NYN	MLB	25	0	1	0	2	0	6[2]	9	1	8.1	6.8	5	35%	.364
2020	NYN	MLB	26	1	2	0	5	5	23	26	5	3.1	5.3	14	42%	.277

Comparables: Luis Cessa, Brandon Woodruff, Jarlin García

After making his major-league debut in 2018, Oswalt had an arm up on the competition and was the first reinforcement called up when the Mets needed a fresh arm early in the season. Of course, the act of needing a fresh arm on April 10 was a portent of things to come for this team and perhaps even more fitting was when that fresh arm walked more batters than he struck out and gave up more than a run per inning. Without overpowering stuff, Oswalt was not seen in the majors after late April, but he did go on to become one of the best pitchers at Triple-A Syracuse.

YEAR	TEAM	LVL	AGE	WHIP	ERA	DRA	WARP	MPH	FB%	WHF	CSP
2017	BIN	AA	23	1.18	2.28	3.44	2.8				
2018	LVG	AAA	24	1.49	6.02	4.21	0.8				
2018	NYN	MLB	24	1.38	5.85	5.73	-0.4	92.9	67	8	47.8
2019	BRO	A-	25	1.50	1.50	5.24	0.0				
2019	SYR	AAA	25	1.14	2.91	3.17	3.0				
2019	NYN	MLB	25	2.25	12.15	5.63	0.0	94.0	65.7	6.6	42
2020	NYN	MLB	26	1.45	5.52	5.64	0.1	92.7	68	8	45.4

David Peterson LHP

Born: 09/03/95   Age: 24   Bats: L   Throws: L
Height: 6'6"   Weight: 240   Origin: Round 1, 2017 Draft (#20 overall)

YEAR	TEAM	LVL	AGE	W	L	SV	G	GS	IP	H	HR	BB/9	K/9	K	GB%	BABIP
2018	COL	A	22	1	4	0	9	9	59[1]	46	1	1.7	8.6	57	68%	.283
2018	SLU	A+	22	6	6	0	13	13	68[2]	74	1	2.5	7.6	58	64%	.335
2019	BIN	AA	23	3	6	0	24	24	116	119	9	2.9	9.5	122	54%	.340
2020	NYN	MLB	24	2	2	0	6	6	32	30	4	3.6	8.0	29	49%	.282

Comparables: Nick Margevicius, Matt Hall, Matt Bowman

Peterson's slider usage increased last season leading to a rise in strikeouts; however, it did not lead to a corresponding increase in his prospect status. The 2017 first-rounder entered the organization with the floor of a back-end starter who can miss enough bats and kill enough worms to see at least a trial run in a major-league rotation, and he's still that now. He'll head to the International League to start 2020 and sits on the cusp of a call-up due to the lack of pitching depth the Mets have in the upper minors.

YEAR	TEAM	LVL	AGE	WHIP	ERA	DRA	WARP	MPH	FB%	WHF	CSP
2018	COL	A	22	0.96	1.82	3.45	1.2				
2018	SLU	A+	22	1.35	4.33	4.89	0.4				
2019	BIN	AA	23	1.34	4.19	5.65	-1.0				
2020	NYN	MLB	24	1.34	4.20	4.47	0.5				

Thomas Szapucki LHP
Born: 06/12/96   Age: 24   Bats: R   Throws: L
Height: 6'2"   Weight: 181   Origin: Round 5, 2015 Draft (#149 overall)

YEAR	TEAM	LVL	AGE	W	L	SV	G	GS	IP	H	HR	BB/9	K/9	K	GB%	BABIP
2017	COL	A	21	1	2	0	6	6	29	24	0	3.1	8.4	27	44%	.304
2019	COL	A	23	0	0	0	11	8	21²	14	1	4.2	10.8	26	37%	.260
2019	SLU	A+	23	1	3	0	9	9	36	33	1	3.8	10.5	42	48%	.314
2020	NYN	MLB	24	2	2	0	33	0	35	34	5	3.5	8.5	33	40%	.293

Comparables: Domingo Germán, Jarlin García, Brad Mills

Szapucki successfully returned to action in 2019 after undergoing Tommy John surgery and missing all of the previous season. The organization very carefully managed his usage as evidenced by the lefty averaging only slightly more than three innings per start. Despite some initial rust, Szapucki put together a successful season across two different leagues and will have a more normal workload as he gets his first taste of the upper minors in 2020.

YEAR	TEAM	LVL	AGE	WHIP	ERA	DRA	WARP	MPH	FB%	WHF	CSP
2017	COL	A	21	1.17	2.79	4.34	0.3				
2019	COL	A	23	1.11	2.08	3.62	0.4				
2019	SLU	A+	23	1.33	3.25	4.69	0.1				
2020	NYN	MLB	24	1.35	4.42	4.65	0.3				

Josh Wolf RHP

Born: 09/01/00   Age: 19   Bats: R   Throws: R
Height: 6'3"   Weight: 170   Origin: Round 2, 2019 Draft (#53 overall)

YEAR	TEAM	LVL	AGE	W	L	SV	G	GS	IP	H	HR	BB/9	K/9	K	GB%	BABIP
2019	MTS	RK	18	0	1	0	5	5	8	9	0	1.1	13.5	12	40%	.450
2020									No projection							

The organization huffed and puffed and blew a good amount of their draft pool allocation on Wolf when they took him in the second round of the 2019 draft and signed him to a $2.15 million bonus—nearly $800,000 over slot. They scraped the bottom of the barrel with senior signs from the fourth through tenth rounds so they could sign both Wolf and third-rounder Matthew Allan to add two promising arms to their system. Wolf's fastball saw a jump in velocity his senior year that he coupled with an above-average curve, making him instantly one of the top pitching prospects in a starved system.

YEAR	TEAM	LVL	AGE	WHIP	ERA	DRA	WARP	MPH	FB%	WHF	CSP
2019	MTS	RK	18	1.25	3.38	3.77	0.2				
2020						No projection					

New York Mets 2020

LINEOUTS

Hitters

HITTER	POS	TEAM	LVL	AGE	PA	R	2B	3B	HR	RBI	BB	K	SB	CS	AVG/OBP/SLG	DRC+	WARP
Aaron Altherr	OF	NYN	MLB	28	35	6	1	0	1	2	2	15	0	0	.129/.200/.258	43	-0.2
	OF	PHI	MLB	28	30	2	1	0	0	1	1	9	0	0	.034/.067/.069	59	-0.1
	OF	SYR	AAA	28	88	9	5	1	4	13	10	16	3	2	.270/.375/.527	115	0.5
	OF	SFN	MLB	28	1	0	0	0	0	0	0	1	0	0	.000/.000/.000	29	0.0
Rajai Davis	LF	SYR	AAA	38	337	47	8	3	8	28	17	72	20	6	.287/.334/.410	91	1.2
	LF	NYN	MLB	38	26	4	2	0	1	8	1	5	0	1	.200/.231/.400	83	-0.1
Sam Haggerty	UT	NYN	MLB	25	4	2	0	0	0	0	0	3	0	0	.000/.000/.000	58	0.0
	UT	BIN	AA	25	292	39	8	5	2	13	40	78	19	4	.259/.370/.356	118	1.7
	UT	BRO	A-	25	25	5	3	0	0	4	4	8	0	0	.333/.440/.476	118	0.2
	UT	SYR	AAA	25	49	9	4	1	1	9	4	10	4	0	.310/.383/.524	106	0.0
Juan Lagares	CF	NYN	MLB	30	285	38	12	1	5	27	22	75	4	1	.213/.279/.326	62	-0.6
Jake Mangum	CF	BRO	A-	23	210	29	5	2	0	18	15	26	17	5	.247/.337/.297	128	1.3
Max Moroff	SS	CLE	MLB	26	35	3	1	0	1	4	2	16	1	0	.125/.176/.250	53	0.0
	SS	COH	AAA	26	136	20	4	0	4	8	26	34	1	2	.213/.375/.361	107	0.6
Jarrett Parker	LF	LAA	MLB	30	15	1	0	0	0	0	3	8	0	0	.000/.200/.000	81	0.0
	LF	SLC	AAA	30	424	71	19	1	24	75	72	125	2	1	.266/.394/.535	114	1.5
Rene Rivera	C	SYR	AAA	35	396	53	13	0	25	73	31	103	0	0	.254/.319/.501	105	2.2
	C	NYN	MLB	35	20	2	0	0	1	3	3	4	0	0	.235/.350/.412	91	0.0
Ali Sanchez	C	SYR	AAA	22	65	5	4	0	0	3	5	11	0	1	.179/.277/.250	57	0.1
	C	BIN	AA	22	294	28	13	0	1	30	23	52	1	0	.278/.337/.337	116	1.7
Mark Vientos	3B	COL	A	19	454	48	27	1	12	62	22	110	1	4	.255/.300/.411	122	1.5

Aaron Altherr's whirlwind tour across three National League teams in 2019 ended with a .300 OPS and an oversized neck brace. ⓧ **Rajai Davis**' debut with the Mets was a memorable day that started with an epic Uber ride from Lehigh Valley and ended with a pinch-hit home run off Sean Doolittle that became one of the more unique highlights of the season. ⓧ **Sam Haggerty** came over in the Kevin Plawecki trade and didn't pick up a hit in four big league at-bats, but his speed made him an ideal pinch-runner. ⓧ **Juan Lagares** had his worst season both at the plate and in the field, which was a troubling development for a team relying on him as one of the few who knew how to play defense. ⓧ **Jake Mangum** is the Mets' fourth-round pick from the 2019 draft. Jeff Mangum is the singer and songwriter from Neutral Milk Hotel. The Dodge Magnum is a two-door coupe produced by Chrysler in the late 1970s. Thomas Magnum is a former navy officer turned private investigator who lives on the island of Oahu. Any questions? ⓧ The Tribe decided they wanted Minimum Moroff after **Max Moroff** logged four hits in 32 at-bats through May 1. ⓧ As an Angel in 2019, **Jarrett Parker** had exactly half as many plate appearance (15) as his age. In baseball's math system, those numbers equate to four—as in Quad-A. ⓧ The Mets have had success with infielders on the international market throughout the decade, but far less so on the grass. They'll look to buck that trend after inking **Alexander Ramirez** to a $2.1 million bonus last summer. He checks a lot of the right boxes as a potential five-tool prospect, but so did Alex Ochoa and Fernando Martínez.

⓫ With the Mets' catching situation so desperate they may as well have lived on Wisteria Lane, it was inevitable that **René Rivera** would be a Met once again after he was released by the Giants. Yet when your homers in Triple A outflank your plate appearances in the majors, it can't really be considered a homecoming.

⓫ **Ali Sanchez** is a defense-first catcher, but offensively he neither floats like a butterfly nor stings like a bee. ⓫ **Mark Vientos** took home the organizational award for the minor-league hitter of the year, and it was well-earned as his offense was 20 percent above league average despite being one of the small group of teenagers in full-season ball.

New York Mets 2020

Pitchers

PITCHER	TEAM	LVL	AGE	W	L	SV	G	GS	IP	H	HR	BB/9	K/9	K	GB%	WHIP	ERA	DRA	WARP
Tyler Bashlor	SYR	AAA	26	3	2	8	33	0	37	29	3	3.6	9.0	37	34%	1.19	3.41	3.36	1.0
	NYN	MLB	26	0	3	0	24	0	22	21	6	7.0	8.2	20	33%	1.73	6.95	7.90	-0.6
Tony Dibrell	SLU	A+	23	8	4	0	17	16	90^1	73	2	3.6	7.6	76	41%	1.21	2.39	3.95	1.2
	BIN	AA	23	0	8	0	9	8	38^2	51	10	4.9	8.6	37	35%	1.86	9.31	8.30	-1.6
Drew Gagnon	SYR	AAA	29	6	5	0	15	15	88^2	78	12	1.7	7.3	72	43%	1.07	2.33	2.98	3.2
	NYN	MLB	29	3	1	0	18	0	23^2	34	11	2.7	6.5	17	40%	1.73	8.37	7.38	-0.5
Ryley Gilliam	SLU	A+	22	0	0	2	7	0	10^2	8	0	1.7	13.5	16	33%	0.94	2.53	2.66	0.3
	BIN	AA	22	3	0	1	12	0	18^2	15	1	3.4	13.5	28	42%	1.18	4.34	3.40	0.3
	SYR	AAA	22	2	0	0	10	0	9^1	19	3	8.7	11.6	12	26%	3.00	13.50	10.07	-0.3
Stephen Gonsalves	TWI	Rk	24	0	1	0	5	5	9	6	2	0.0	16.0	16	35%	0.67	2.00	0.42	0.5
Harol Gonzalez	BIN	AA	24	6	4	0	17	16	97^1	83	12	2.1	8.2	89	46%	1.09	3.14	4.26	0.8
	SYR	AAA	24	6	0	0	8	7	40^1	33	8	2.2	5.1	23	44%	1.07	2.68	3.69	1.2
Donnie Hart	SAN	AAA	28	4	3	3	40	0	37^1	43	3	3.1	7.2	30	57%	1.50	4.10	4.10	0.8
	SYR	AAA	28	0	0	0	8	0	7^1	11	2	1.2	3.7	3	47%	1.64	6.14	5.43	0.1
	MIL	MLB	28	0	0	0	4	0	6^2	4	0	5.4	4.1	3	68%	1.20	0.00	5.30	0.0
	NYN	MLB	28	0	0	0	1	0	1	0	0	0.0	0.0	0	100%	0.00	0.00	3.35	0.0
Walker Lockett	SLU	A+	25	1	0	0	2	2	7	8	1	0.0	7.7	6	52%	1.14	5.14	4.15	0.1
	SYR	AAA	25	3	3	0	11	10	59	75	5	1.7	5.9	39	56%	1.46	3.66	4.44	1.3
	NYN	MLB	25	1	1	0	9	4	22^2	33	6	2.4	6.4	16	42%	1.72	8.34	4.96	0.2
Stephen Nogosek	BIN	AA	24	0	0	1	11	0	19	13	0	5.7	9.5	20	35%	1.32	0.95	4.57	0.0
	SYR	AAA	24	3	0	2	24	0	31^1	12	1	3.7	8.6	30	38%	0.80	1.15	1.83	1.3
	NYN	MLB	24	0	1	0	7	0	6^2	12	2	2.7	8.1	6	38%	2.10	10.80	6.23	-0.1
Pedro Payano	FRI	AA	24	3	1	0	8	8	42^2	30	3	3.8	10.3	49	43%	1.12	4.43	3.32	0.9
	NAS	AAA	24	2	3	0	11	10	41^1	42	8	6.1	9.6	44	38%	1.69	5.44	6.97	-0.1
	TEX	MLB	24	1	2	0	6	4	22	26	3	6.1	7.0	17	47%	1.86	5.73	7.39	-0.4
Tim Peterson	SYR	AAA	28	2	6	9	41	0	55	42	7	2.1	8.8	54	33%	1.00	2.95	2.66	1.9
	NYN	MLB	28	0	0	0	6	0	7^1	7	1	8.6	3.7	3	25%	1.91	4.91	5.40	0.0
Brooks Pounders	COH	AAA	28	2	1	1	24	0	35	19	4	2.8	11.8	46	42%	0.86	2.31	4.64	0.5
	SYR	AAA	28	1	2	0	19	1	21^1	29	4	3.8	8.4	20	30%	1.78	7.59	4.96	0.3
	NYN	MLB	28	1	0	0	7	0	7^1	9	1	2.5	6.1	5	42%	1.50	6.14	6.19	-0.1
Nick Rumbelow	SYR	AAA	27	0	0	0	5	0	6^1	11	1	2.8	8.5	6	44%	2.05	4.26	6.10	0.0
	TAC	AAA	27	3	2	0	19	0	25^1	37	5	5.3	7.8	22	47%	2.05	8.17	7.62	-0.3
	SEA	MLB	27	0	0	1	3	0	1^1	3	2	6.8	13.5	2	17%	3.00	27.00	6.52	0.0
Ervin Santana	SLU	A+	36	1	1	0	3	3	13	15	2	2.1	7.6	11	58%	1.38	4.85	5.55	-0.1
	SYR	AAA	36	4	4	0	15	15	82	97	11	3.5	5.9	54	39%	1.57	5.38	5.98	0.6
	CHA	MLB	36	0	2	0	3	3	13^1	19	6	4.1	3.4	5	32%	1.88	9.45	9.25	-0.5
Junior Santos	KNG	Rk+	17	0	5	0	14	14	40^2	46	4	5.5	8.0	36	31%	1.75	5.09	7.00	-0.3
Kevin Smith	SLU	A+	22	5	5	0	17	17	85^2	83	5	2.5	10.7	102	45%	1.25	3.05	4.32	0.7
	BIN	AA	22	3	2	0	6	6	31^1	25	1	4.3	8.0	28	40%	1.28	3.45	5.60	-0.2
Daniel Zamora	SYR	AAA	26	2	1	4	29	0	30	26	1	2.1	10.8	36	47%	1.10	4.20	2.70	1.0
	NYN	MLB	26	0	1	0	17	0	8^2	10	1	5.2	8.3	8	30%	1.73	5.19	7.63	-0.2

For a person with "bash" in their last name **Tyler Bashlor** couldn't help but become a self-fulfilling prophecy last season by allowing nearly 2.5 homers per nine innings. It's not what you want. ⓥ **Tony Dibrell** pitched effectively enough to earn a promotion to Double-A, but the walks that had plagued him throughout his young career found him again in Binghamton, adding up to disastrous results for the 23-year-old. ⓥ After a few good outings, **Drew Gagnon** was mistakenly placed in manager Mickey Callaway's circle of trust only for it to blow up spectacularly. This is also a summary for how his appearances went after May. ⓥ **Ryley Gilliam** was a fast riser through the system, features an above-average fastball and sports an 80-grade baseball name. ⓥ A year after losing his fastball location and any semblance of bat-missing, **Stephen Gonsalves** missed just about the entire season with a strained elbow. ⓥ **Harol Gonzalez** was a borderline non-prospect heading into the season after struggling in Double-A without overpowering stuff, but he was significantly better the second time around, participated in a combined no-hitter and continued to thrive after getting a promotion to Syracuse. ⓥ **Donnie Hart** doesn't wear his sunglasses at night because he is Donnie and not Corey. He also throws sidearm and pitched exactly one inning for the Mets last season. ⓥ **Jordan Humphreys** has missed most of the last two-and-a-half seasons due to things related to Tommy John surgery. He was emerging into a pretty good prospect before he was felled back in 2017, and the Mets saw enough in the Arizona Fall League to add him to the 40-man roster in November. ⓥ The Mets seemingly made a shrewd move when they acquired **Franklyn Kilome** for Asdrúbal Cabrera in 2018, so naturally he underwent Tommy John and missed the entire 2019 season. ⓥ **Walker Lockett** was traded for catcher Kevin Plawecki and pitched to an 8.34 ERA for the Mets whereas Plawecki had an elite 0.00 ERA in relief for Cleveland. So who won the trade? It's hard to say really. ⓥ **Stephen Nogosek** had an amazing year if you ignore everything he did at the major-league level. ⓥ **Pedro Payano** pairs a low-to-mid-90s sinker with a slider that generated whiffs on more than half the swings taken against it during his big-league cameo. So far as minor-league signings go, he's one worth watching. ⓥ Homer-prone **Tim Peterson** is the kind of generic Triple-A relief arm that has gotten pressed into up-and-down duty as pitching staffs have expanded and teams have gotten aggressive about cycling optionable pitchers. ⓥ Between his great name and stout frame, **Brooks Pounders** is a BIG BOY SZN meme waiting to happen, if only he could pitch well enough to hang around in the majors for a bit. It didn't happen in 2019 and it probably won't in 2020. ⓥ If history proves any guide, **Nick Rumbelow**'s signing with a New York franchise in the winter augurs a trade to Seattle by the next offseason for a prospect who the Mariners will pay more to reacquire in two years' time. ⓥ Signing a player with the last name of Santana who had thrown a no-hitter in his career seemed like a good idea at the time, but **Ervin Santana** struggled mightily in the minors and luckily for the Mets the veteran was never needed to plug holes. ⓥ **Junior Santos** stood head and shoulders above his competition last season. At 6-foot-8 and 218 pounds he had a commanding

presence on the mound coupled with a fastball that sat in the mid-90s. As a teen, he still has room to grow which is a terrifying thought for opposing batters. ⚾
Drew Smith remains the most promising arm the Mets managed to get back at the 2017 trade deadline, and he was sidelined all season after undergoing Tommy John surgery. ⚾ **Kevin Smith** won the organization's award for pitcher of the year after becoming a full-time starter last season, and did not give up a home run to a lefty despite pitching nearly 120 innings. ⚾ **Daniel Zamora** once threw only sliders in a nine-pitch at-bat that ended in a walk.

Mets Prospects

The State of the System

The Mets system is improved at the top due to an aggressive 2019 draft strategy, but the overall talent is still very thin and most of these names are far away from Flushing.

The Top Ten

1 ★ ★ ★ *2020 Top 101 Prospect* **#48** ★ ★ ★
Ronny Mauricio   SS   OFP: 60   ETA: 2021
Born: 04/04/01   Age: 19   Bats: B   Throws: R   Height: 6'3"   Weight: 166
Origin: International Free Agent, 2017

The Report: This is what it's supposed to look like at 18 years old. There's real-deal, first-division ability here regardless of future position. Our confidence in that comes mostly from a potential plus hit tool, advanced feel for the barrel, and above-average-to-plus bat speed. It's a loose, easy stroke with good hands and commensurate feel for contact, and it's downright pretty when his lower half syncs and fires effectively. Mauricio relies on his raw feel at times, because he's overly aggressive and can get out of sync, especially if you bust him inside.

Mauricio's power is mostly projection right now, but there's a lot of room to grow into impact pop. A bat path tweak for increased loft paired with his feel to hit would mean plus game power. Mauricio's soft hands, smooth actions, and easy plus arm would work anywhere in the infield, but the book is still out on his range as he fills out. He's currently rangy enough to stay at shortstop, but dropping a tick there could signal a move to third, where his defensive profile could grade out as plus. He's a solid athlete and an average runner underway but is below-average down the line. Mauricio has the makings of a mashing infielder with four consistent tools and tons of projection. Although he's just 18, this is what an org's number one prospect looks like.

Variance: High. There's confidence that the bat will play and power will come, but an aggressive eye will present a challenge or two along the way, and he just finished his first full season.

Ben Carsley's Fantasy Take: Yes, please. Any time you can tease me with plus-power/plus-hit projection I'll pay attention, and that's doubly true when we're talking about an infielder. It's reasonable to have visions of a .280 hitter with 25-30 bombs dancing in your head. The only issue here is lead time; even if Mauricio does reach the aggressive MLB ETA cited above, I'd argue his true fantasy impact ETA is closer to 2022 or beyond. Still, we snuck Mauricio into the "Honorable Mentions" section of our Top 101 list a year ago, and I wish we'd been even more aggressive now. Basically, this is my way of saying "sorry, Bret (but now we're even for Robert Gsellman)."

―――― ★ ★ ★ *2020 Top 101 Prospect* **#88** ★ ★ ★ ――――

2 Francisco Alvarez   C   OFP: 60   ETA: 2023
Born: 11/19/01   Age: 18   Bats: R   Throws: R   Height: 5'11"   Weight: 220
Origin: International Free Agent, 2018

The Report: One should always proceed with caution when projecting great things of a player just past most of the world's legal drinking age—and ranking him as such—but Álvarez was rated highly as an international signee and has done nothing but improve his standing early in his pro career. He put up very good numbers as a 17-year-old in the Appy League, which would be surprising if not for his natural hitting talent and advanced approach at the dish. Álvarez has an advanced, patient approach already and waits for his pitch to drive. There is a deadly controlled aggression to his swing, and power is already showing up in games thanks to well above-average bat speed and his strength, which is visible throughout his frame.

As for that frame, it is a stocky one and lacking in physical projection. To my eye, it's perfect for a catcher as long as he can maintain it where it is. Álvarez is very comfortable behind the plate, too, athletic enough to handle bad breakers in the dirt, and he shows a quick trigger out of the crouch that allows his above-average arm to play up. The receiving appears advanced for his age, and he takes charge with his pitchers. It is early yet but this is a very well-rounded and advanced catching profile that has the teenager living up to his hype.

Variance: High. Álvarez is about as safe a bet as there is among teenagers just off the complexes, but that really isn't saying much. There's still a lot of development in front of him, both behind the plate and next to it.

Ben Carsley's Fantasy Take: At the risk of being inflexible, I just refuse to buy in on teenage catching prospects anymore. Too much can go wrong, and even if things go right eventually, we tend to be way off in our fantasy impact ETAs. If you still believe in catching prospects then the time to get in on Álvarez is now. If you're like me, well, you'll hang a picture of Francisco Mejia next to your bed as a reminder not to get sucked in by toolsy guys like Álvarez. Unless he's Prime Buster Posey, Álvarez (and guys like him are) is just not worth punting a roster spot for four or five years before he starts returning any value.

★ ★ ★ *2020 Top 101 Prospect* #90 ★ ★ ★

3 Andrés Giménez SS   OFP: 50   ETA: Late 2020
Born: 09/04/98   Age: 21   Bats: L   Throws: R   Height: 6'0"   Weight: 161
Origin: International Free Agent, 2015

The Report: Giménez scuffled in a return engagement with the Eastern League. The Mets tweaked his swing for more power, and the results were less than ideal. He did scrape a few more over the fence, and he did flash another half grade of power at five o'clock, but at the cost of increased swing-and-miss and worse quality of contact overall. Giménez was routinely late on fastballs away, and struggled to deal with left-on-left spin. What was previously a plus hit tool projection now looks fringier, which could be a major blow to the overall profile. The staff reports on him from the Fall League were better, as he seems to at least be more comfortable with the tweaks, but I'm still concerned until I see it work somewhere else than the surface of the moon against gassed pitchers.

The good news is the speed and glove are still intact. Giménez is a present above-average shortstop, with more than enough arm for the left side of the diamond. More game reps could easily smooth things out further and make him plus there. He's a plus, borderline plus-plus runner, although his baserunning can be a bit rough at times. If he smooths out the swing, or goes back to what worked for him in 2020, this might all seem overly reactive. Sometimes you just have a year, but it was a bad year.

Variance: Medium. The glove gives Giménez a reasonable bench floor, but the hit tool variance is worrisome now for a player who can lack physicality at the plate at times.

Ben Carsley's Fantasy Take: Ehhhhh. I'm usually a sucker for speed-first infielders, but Giménez doesn't really do it for me. It's great that he's a lock to stick at short, and the relatively short lead time gives him an argument to still serve as a top-101 dynasty prospect. He should be at the very back of that list if he makes it at all, though, and I'm concerned enough that I get real Orlando Arcia vibes from the overall profile. It's reasonable to be higher on Giménez than I am given the previous aptitude he showed with the bat, but this is not exactly the Age of Reason.

4 Matthew Allan RHP   OFP: 50   ETA: 2022-23
Born: 04/17/01   Age: 19   Bats: R   Throws: R   Height: 6'3"   Weight: 225
Origin: Round 3, 2019 Draft (#89 overall)

The Report: Allan was widely considered one of the top prep pitchers in the 2019 class, but was floating a large bonus demand that caused him to fall. Jeff Passan of ESPN reported during the draft that the Cubs almost selected him with the 27th pick, but went elsewhere because of signability. (Their actual pick there,

Ryan Jensen, later signed for a below-slot $2 million.) The Mets took him in the third round, and made room for his $2.5 million bonus by selecting a slew of extremely cheap senior signs in rounds 4-10.

Is Allan worth it? That'll take a solid four or five years to work out, but early signs are positive. He looked the part in his abbreviated pro debut, popping up in short-season Brooklyn for their Penn League title run and throwing a consistent 95-96. His out pitch is a plus curveball, and his changeup projects out to at least average. It's a strong mix of stuff and relative polish, and we like him enough that we have him ahead of actual first-rounder Brett Baty on the current organizational ranking and in the mix for the bottom of the 101. Yet the risk of investing this heavily in prep pitching is the same as it ever was.

Variance: Very high. He's an 18-year-old pitcher who has yet to pitch in full-season ball. Things can go in many, many, many directions from here.

Ben Carsley's Fantasy Take: Don't let Allan fall off your radar just because he was popped later than some of the other big-name prep arms from this draft class; he's got the goods. While I don't foresee him ranking anywhere near the dynasty version of our top-101, he's in the next, meaty glut of high-upside arms who essentially amount to shiny lottery tickets for our purposes. If you play with less seasoned dynasty leaguers who are likely to only look at first-round hitters in their supplemental drafts, Allan could provide you with some nice value late.

5 — Brett Baty   3B

OFP: 55   ETA: 2023
Born: 11/13/99   Age: 20   Bats: L   Throws: R   Height: 6'3"   Weight: 210
Origin: Round 1, 2019 Draft (#12 overall)

The Report: Baty's profile is the type that will create splits of opinion resulting in widely varied outcome projections and wildly controversial rankings. There are those who see an already advanced bat who will quickly conquer each level and alleviate concerns about other parts of his game. It is well known that Baty was on the older end of draft-eligible high-schoolers, and the importance of this fact is of course up for debate. Detractors might also point to his very developed body that leans toward negative physical projection more than anything else, or to his underwhelming athleticism and feel for the hot corner. I got a quick glance near the end of his Appy League campaign and noted roughly these same positives and negatives. He's a mature hitter with excellent plate discipline, and this held true even as he was struggling to find his footing following his promotion off the complex. His power is real too, plus to all fields. In fact, his approach the other way is quite good and he has an impressive ability to wait back on breaking stuff and drive it. It concerned me slightly that despite the bat speed he swung through some fastballs and I didn't really see him pull anything with authority, though it was eight or ten plate appearances and the latter part seemed mostly by design.

Variance: High. He really needs to hit and he hasn't yet, though that doesn't mean he won't. He'll have to hit even more if it ends up that he's a first baseman, which is a possibility.

Ben Carsley's Fantasy Take: I, too, have a "very developed body that leans toward negative physical projection," but at least writing with Craig keeps me from being old for my level. Anyway, Baty is a better dynasty prospect than real life prospect because he should move relatively quickly and because his bat is his best tool. That being said, he comes with just enough risk that he's a fringier dynasty asset than this draft position might indicate. It's a very Maikel Franco profile, for better and for worse.

6 Mark Vientos   3B
OFP: 55   ETA: 2022
Born: 12/11/99   Age: 20   Bats: R   Throws: R   Height: 6'4"   Weight: 185
Origin: Round 2, 2017 Draft (#59 overall)

The Report: Already a somewhat polarizing prospect, it can be hard to believe that Vientos is still only 19 and (age-appropriately) submerged in the low minors. Vientos has made a good impression with the bat all things considered, winning an organizational award this season despite tailing off as the campaign neared its conclusion. His best tool is his raw power, which is easily plus and already more than viable in game. The hit tool is a little more questionable, as there is some swing-and-miss in his long levers, and the approach is a little aggressive at present. There are positives though, like his all-fields approach and ability to wait back on and drive breaking stuff. Vientos has a wiry strong frame with some physical projection remaining in the upper body and possesses good overall athleticism. His arm is just shy of plus, the best feature of a defensive profile that is more or less fringe-average. How his story is written will largely depend on where he can get his hit tool, and how much of his power it allows him to tap into. Still young, Vientos has plenty of time to shape the narrative.

Variance: High. Questions about the hit tool still exist and as a corner bat who is only decent defensively he'll need it, even with the power.

Ben Carsley's Fantasy Take: Anyone else getting Michael Chavis flashbacks? Despite the flaws in his game, I actually like Vientos more than the two prospects listed above him in this non-dynasty list. The power is real, I think he can stick at third unless usurped by a much better option, and the ETA is fantasy-friendly. He's probably not a top-101 dude at this point, but you can make an argument for him as top-150. Don't let the prospect fatigue set in just yet.

7 Josh Wolf   RHP
OFP: 55   ETA: 2024
Born: 09/01/00   Age: 19   Bats: R   Throws: R   Height: 6'3"   Weight: 170
Origin: Round 2, 2019 Draft (#53 overall)

The Report: The Mets went back to the Texas prep arm well for their second round pick last summer, after popping Simeon Woods Richardson in 2018. The two are actually fairly comparable on their respective draft days, although Wolf is the more traditional tall, lean, projectable Lone Star arm. Both were velocity pop-up guys their senior year of high school, as Wolf came out touching 98. Both feature advanced, big breaking 11-6 curveballs. Wolf has gotten better marks for pitchability, but the delivery has more reliever markers, and he lacks Woods Richardson's plus athleticism on the mound. On the other hand, given his thin frame, Wolf might be more likely to sit mid 90s as a starter if he fills out and adds arm strength in his twenties. He'll need to stay healthy and develop a changeup and so on and so forth, but he is an intriguing power arm for a system sorely lacking in interesting pitching prospects.

Variance: Very high. The track record of prep righties taken outside of the first round is not amazing. There's the usual third pitch concerns at present.

Ben Carsley's Fantasy Take: Wolf is a bit too far away for me to get truly excited at this point, but I do like him a bit more than the plethora of righties with decent upsides who occupy the back halves of most of these lists. Maybe it's because I'm a sucker for curveballs? Or Wolves? Either way, he's a good one for your watch list.

8   David Peterson   LHP   OFP: 50   ETA: Second half 2020
Born: 09/03/95   Age: 24   Bats: L   Throws: L   Height: 6'6"   Weight: 240
Origin: Round 1, 2017 Draft (#20 overall)

The Report: Peterson more or less held serve as a prospect in 2019. Double-A wasn't much of a test for his array of average-ish stuff, although he was occasionally too hittable due to his command being not fine enough. He's a tall, extra-large lefty with a tough angle due to his extension, crossfire, and three-quarters slot. His fastball sits in the low 90s and he can turn it over with some arm-side run, or bore it in to righties. His slider is his best secondary, a low-80s, two-plane breaker that he commands well. It's an above-average offering that flashes better, but lacks the true "hard slider" characteristics to be consistently plus. The changeup is the third pitch, inconsistent and often firm, but showing good sink in the low 80s when he pulls the string. Peterson has never really dominated to the level you'd expect from a first-round college arm, but he has a solid frame built to log innings, and enough stuff to get major league hitters out. It's just a very average profile overall.

Variance: Medium. He was fine in Double-A, and while there will be lingering concerns about a major league out pitch until he's getting major leaguers out, he's a polished lefty with a solid slider. That usually plays.

Ben Carsley's Fantasy Take: "What if Wade Miley, but taller?" just isn't a very enticing fantasy proposition. Peterson is a fine speculative grab if you need 2020 innings or if your league rosters 300-plus prospects. So are about 20 other dudes with this profile, and many of them at least have a hint of upside and/or guaranteed rotation spots.

9 **Junior Santos   RHP**   OFP: 55   ETA: 2023-24
Born: 08/16/01   Age: 18   Bats: R   Throws: R   Height: 6'8"   Weight: 218
Origin: International Free Agent, 2018

The Report: Santos may be a young'un—he was born a month before *Yankee Hotel Foxtrot* came out—but the Mets have pushed him hard as a pro. After signing for 150k, he came stateside in 2018 as soon as he was 17, and spent almost the entire summer in Kingsport unable to legally purchase Marlboros (or I guess vape juice or whatever the kids are huffing now). Santos doesn't look like literally a child though, as he's already a huge human, probably at least 20 pounds bigger than his listed weight, but still physically projectable. The delivery is a little stiff at present, but he keeps all the limbs in mostly good order throughout. And when the baseball comes out of the child's hands it's mid-90s heat touching as high as 98—although the velo can be inconsistent. There's feel for a potentially above-average breaking ball as well. Look, Santos posted a 5+ ERA in the Appy, and this could go in a bunch of different directions in the coming years—many of them involving three spent eating fried seafood at Lola's in St. Lucie, a conversion to the pen, maybe a Tommy John surgery. But it's a quality frame with projection and better stuff and more polish than you'd expect from a teenager. In this system, grab every lottery ticket you can.

Variance: Extreme. He was 17 for most of the year and not particularly efficient in the Appy. He might never get out of A-ball, he might be the best pitching prospect in the system next year.

Ben Carsley's Fantasy Take: Check back in five years, at which point Santos might be in Low-A.

10 **Thomas Szapucki   LHP**   OFP: 50   ETA: 2021
Born: 06/12/96   Age: 24   Bats: R   Throws: L   Height: 6'2"   Weight: 181
Origin: Round 5, 2015 Draft (#149 overall)

The Report: Szapucki got a slow start to 2019, eighteen months off Tommy John surgery. Reports from St. Lucie in March suggested he wasn't really stretched out enough to break camp, but the Mets sent him north to Columbia anyway, where he topped out in the low 90s and quickly got a one-month breather. He's slowly built up arm strength since then and earned a July promotion to High-A. Later reports have the fastball touching 95, and Szapucki showing an improved curve, but this is still a ways off from the mid-90s and potential plus-plus breaker he showed in 2016. The changeup is still below average. Szapucki struggles to hold that stuff even 50 pitches into games and only threw 61 innings across 22 outings this season. This looks like a bad rehab at present, but even 75 percent of the stuff he used to have is an average fastball and above-average curveball in short bursts. You can play the waiting game a bit longer here—he's left-handed with a good frame—but the Mets have had enough bad TJ rehabs in recent years that it might not just be bad luck.

Variance: Very High. Szapucki's stuff hasn't fully come back now two-plus years off Tommy John, and there were durability questions about him before the UCL tear. He'll be 24 next year and has made one start above A-ball. We'd like to bet on the stuff that once made him a Top 101 arm, but we'll need to see it back in games first.

Ben Carsley's Fantasy Take: I know you might be tempted to want to buy low on Szapucki given his former rankings, but the risk-to-reward ratio here is all wrong. You can keep an eye on him for a quick pickup if the stuff looks like it's back, but right now Szapucki should be unowned in all but the very deepest of dynasty leagues. Odds are the Mets fan in your league still wants him, though!

The Next Ten

11 **Shervyen Newton   IF**
Born: 04/24/99   Age: 21   Bats: B   Throws: R   Height: 6'4"   Weight: 180
Origin: International Free Agent, 2015

Newton's frame and tools are really loud. He looks the part with a high waist, present strength and tons of projection in a lengthy frame, but he's also a solid athlete with smooth actions in the field to help his tools translate. That feel shows at the plate, too, with a sound swing from the left side featuring excellent lift and separation with flashes of a solid eye and plus bat speed. The question is whether he can tone down the swing-and-miss and bouts of over-aggressiveness. He'll grow out of the middle infield to become a solid, athletic corner defender at third or right with a plus arm and potential double-plus raw power. The risk here is extreme as a boom-or-bust type who needs the hit tool to come along, but the ceiling is equally extreme with big projection, big pop and big athleticism.

12 **Franklyn Kilomé   RHP**
Born: 06/25/95   Age: 25   Bats: R   Throws: R   Height: 6'6"   Weight: 175
Origin: International Free Agent, 2013

Kilomé missed all of 2019 recovering from Tommy John surgery, and still comes in as the sixth-best pitching prospect in the Mets system. That says plenty about the pitching depth here, but also a little bit about Kilomé's upside. He flashed better command of his stuff at the end of 2018, and while a reliever outcome is far more likely now—Kilomé will be turning 25 next season and hasn't pitched above Double-A—there's near-term late-inning impact potential the Mets don't have anywhere else in the system. Kilomé could be 95+ with a 7 curveball from a tough angle for hitters. There's very high risk here, though, and the Mets don't have a great recent track record with Tommy John recoveries.

/gestures further up the list to Thomas Szapucki.

/pours one out for Marcos Molina.

13 **Jaylen Palmer   IF**
Born: 07/31/00   Age: 19   Bats: R   Throws: R   Height: 6'3"   Weight: 195
Origin: Round 22, 2018 Draft (#650 overall)

"Next year's Shervyen Newton" had a very 2018 Shervyen Newton season in the Appy. So far, so good. Well, there's some bad in there, like significant swing-and-miss. Palmer generates good bat speed out of a lean, athletic frame, but the swing path is long and steep. As he fills out the power should come—and his seven bombs this summer is already a good showing for an 18-year-old outside of the complex—but how much of it plays in games will be an open question for, oh a half decade or so. He's played third base and short so far as a pro, but is likely to end up at third as he fills out, assuming he stays on the dirt—Palmer could be an interesting center field candidate at some point. There's a lot of *could be's* in the profile, and like with a lot of the Mets system—including Shervyen Newton still—you are betting on an athletic body and some loud tools. Worse parlays to make, one supposes, and often better than the alternatives on this list.

14 **Kevin Smith   LHP**
Born: 05/13/97   Age: 23   Bats: R   Throws: L   Height: 6'5"   Weight: 200
Origin: Round 7, 2018 Draft (#200 overall)

If there was a breakout performance in the Mets system in 2019—at least among prospects they didn't trade away at the deadline—it might have been Kevin Smith. The 2018 seventh-round pick posted a solid ERA and strong K rates at two levels. The stuff doesn't match the numbers, though, as Smith sits either side of 90. Smith is, at least, a tall lefty with a long stride and good extension on the fastball, and it's a high spin offering. There's a slurvy breaker that's tough left-on-left due to the angle he creates, and the changeup will flash average fade. Smith generally keeps everything down in the zone despite fringe command, but we'll need to see a longer track record of success and quality strike throwing in the upper minors before we throw a backend starter OFP on him, since the profile is fringy overall.

15 **Stephen Gonsalves   LHP**
Born: 07/08/94   Age: 25   Bats: L   Throws: L   Height: 6'5"   Weight: 220
Origin: Round 4, 2013 Draft (#110 overall)

It's not a great sign when a 25-year-old waiver claim who missed almost all of 2019 with an elbow strain is making your prospect list. That said he fits right in with this tier of Mets prospect arms in that regard, and when healthy Gonsalves projected as a quality back-of-the-rotation option with four fringe-to-above-average pitches. It's overly simplistic to call him "Kevin Smith with better secondaries," but the deliveries and fastballs aren't that dissimilar. Gonsalves has a tick more velo if anything, touching 93 in his late season appearances, and has flashed an above-average change and slider/cutter thing at times. Smith is healthy, Gonsalves hasn't been—although he has a clean bill of health at the time of publication—and neither would be as high in even an average system. The Mets—as you may have gathered by now—are not an average system.

16 Freddy Valdez OF
Born: 12/06/01 Age: 18 Bats: R Throws: R Height: 6'3" Weight: 212
Origin: International Free Agent, 2018

Valdez was held back in the Dominican Summer League this summer and ended up playing the bulk of the season two levels behind Álvarez, his fellow seven-figure 2018 J2 signing. It's not like it's a true negative for a 17-year-old to spend the year in the international complex and come stateside for a late cameo, but it does indicate he's on a slower track. Frankly, he fits the criteria for high profile international signings who tend to be overrated in this period of their prospectdom. The scouting reports that would've gotten him said seven-figure bonus are years old now, and teams tend to pay for early physical development because of how early players are (illegally) agreeing to terms. Valdez has barely even been exposed to domestic complex level pitching yet, so it's hard to figure out what to make of him as a pro outside of generic "future power hitter" platitudes. Then again, he's just behind a waiver claim on this list, and just ahead of a back-end starter exposed to Rule 5 and a pitcher coming off two years off for Tommy John, so we'll call his placement an artifact of a very thin system.

17 Harol Gonzalez RHP
Born: 03/02/95 Age: 25 Bats: B Throws: R Height: 6'0" Weight: 160
Origin: International Free Agent, 2014

I was fully expecting to pen a fun little riff on Harol Gonzalez in the personal cheeseball section below. My affinity for him dates back to the first piece I ever wrote for BP. If there is any prospect in baseball I root to outperform my projection, it's Harol. But the projection has never been all that rosy. The undersized righty has added some bulk and a few ticks on the fastball. He now sits low 90s with occasional cut or arm-side wiggle. I even got a report he touched 95. The curve has gotten to average, as he manipulates the shape and commands the pitch well, although it can roll into the lefty happy zone at times. Harol's slider/cutter thing never really developed though, and the changeup has stagnated. It's a collection of fringe offerings with some pitchability and command, but long ball issues even before he got the Triple-A ball in his hands. Yet here he sits in the Next Ten, because this system is so shallow that being both reasonably close to the majors and with a shot to be a fifth starter or swingman made it challenging to find 20 prospects I preferred, even with my biases set aside. The Mets don't seem to agree, so I won't be shocked if he gets popped in the Rule 5 and ends up a bulk innings guy behind somebody's opener in 2021, although you'd prefer to be able to shuttle this profile back and forth from Triple-A.

18. Jordan Humphreys   RHP
Born: 06/11/96   Age: 24   Bats: R   Throws: R   Height: 6'2"   Weight: 223
Origin: Round 18, 2015 Draft (#539 overall)

Speaking of problematic Tommy John rehabs, Humphreys missed two full seasons after mid-2017 surgery, popping up once in June and once in August for complex appearances. Seems bad. He looked fine in the AFL, sitting low 90s and touching 96 and flashing a decent slider and change, which jibes with our 2017 looks, albeit with a different breaker popping. There was fairly significant relief risk in the profile even then, and that's only increased with the lost development time. Humphreys will be 24 next year and has thrown 11 innings above the South Atlantic League. Nevertheless the Mets added him to the 40-man for Rule 5 protection. He could move quickly with a full-time shift to the pen in 2020, although there's an argument that he still needs starter's innings for development reasons, even if he's not too likely to be a long term rotation piece. There's setup potential as a reliever, but the variance here is, uh, significant.

19. Sebastian Espino   IF
Born: 05/29/00   Age: 20   Bats: R   Throws: R   Height: 6'2"   Weight: 176
Origin: International Free Agent, 2016

There are probably dudes with a higher floor who could fill this slot, but there are enough positive traits here to elevate Espino into the discussion. A mid-level international signing a few years ago now, the 19-year-old shortstop has put up mediocre offensive numbers that I would argue are not commensurate with his talents. The stats basically reflect weaknesses that are easy to pick up in a couple looks. He's long, lean, and very physically projectible but the power just isn't there yet, although of course it isn't guaranteed to ever get there. But he is quick to the ball in spite of his long arms, and can jump a fastball in his zone. He will swing and miss, one might say too much, at breaking stuff especially. While he might be a work in progress at the plate, his defensive work is quite impressive. He is silky at the six, with good action and reactions and more than enough range and arm. A lot of what I like here is tangled up in offensive production, but there are worse prospects to have in the corner of your eye.

20. Daison Acosta   RHP
Born: 08/24/98   Age: 21   Bats: R   Throws: R   Height: 6'2"   Weight: 160
Origin: International Free Agent, 2016

A great example of the type of prospect who can pop up when you have room for a few extra in your lower minors (he signed for only $70K in 2016), Acosta is lean and projectible at 6-foot-2 and a listed 160. He's 92-94 from a low-effort three-quarters motion and complements the fastball with a strong slider around 80 mph that has late, sharp bite. Interestingly, the night I saw him he seemed to be experimenting with a cutter-like pitch around 86-88 that turned out to be very effective. It was a dark and stormy night and difficult to tell what sort of effect the mound conditions were having on pitch selection, but it appeared to be an interesting wrinkle in between his two bread and butter offerings. He's probably ready to begin his age-21 season at High-A, and in a system such as this he's worth following. If the cutter is a mirage he's more likely a two-pitch guy and quite possibly a reliever, but if he's in that role and making noise at the upper levels in a couple years the Mets will definitely be able to use him.

Personal Cheeseball

PC

Stephen Villines   RHP
Born: 07/15/95   Age: 24   Bats: R   Throws: R   Height: 6'2"   Weight: 175
Origin: Round 10, 2017 Draft (#307 overall)

There was a serial comic that ran in *SI for Kids* in the 1990s. I only half-remember most of it, and there's a non-zero chance it's part of some odd Mandela Effect. I think it was set in the 1950s—I recall a bunch of deep V-neck cricket sweaters—but I do distinctly remember one story arc that featured a nerdy kind of sports fan who discovered he was a very good junkballing pitcher. He leads his team to the state championship or something where he faces some jockish lout from their rival in the ninth inning. Our protagonist thinks to himself, "If he's going to beat me he's going to have to hit my best fastball." The next panel narration announces, "And he does, for a HOME RUN!" Steve Villines' ethos on the mound was to throw his best fastball and dare minor league batters to hit it. His fastball, mind you, is mid 80s from a sidearm slot. Up until a midseason promotion to Triple-A, no one could. But our humble 90s comics narrator came for Villines as he gave up 23 hits and four home runs in 16 innings for Syracuse. Villines does throw a short frisbee slider, and his change has flashed at times, although not for a while. But mostly he just tries to beat guys with that fastball. I appreciate the *joie de vivre* inherent in just shoving 86 mph in the faces of the best hitters on the planet and daring them to mash it, but that didn't even work long in the funny pages

Low Minors Sleeper

LMS

Jordany Ventura   RHP
Born: 07/06/00   Age: 19   Bats: R   Throws: R   Height: 6'0"   Weight: 162
Origin: International Free Agent, 2018

Ventura wasn't a big name out of the Dominican Republic and sort of came out of nowhere last year as a 19-year-old to begin blurring the edges of the radar. He was just up from Florida when I saw him on the August Appy circuit sitting low 90s with a well-developing curve in the upper 70s with an interesting change trailing behind. The breaker has sharp bite and is pretty true, around 11-5, and he can throw it for strikes. I said the change was trailing behind but that is due more to the strength of the curve than the weakness of his third pitch, which has some nice split action and drew some rough passes. The heater might not sound overpowering but there's some natural cut to it and the broad-shouldered Ventura is very physically projectible. Listed at 6-foot but looking taller up on the mound, he has a solid motion with a very high three-quarters release point that he repeats well enough for an average to above command projection. It will be interesting to see if the Mets push him to full season ball when next season begins, because there is a fair amount to like here.

Top Talents 25 and Under (as of 4/1/2020)

1. Pete Alonso
2. Amed Rosario
3. Dominic Smith
4. Ronny Mauricio
5. Francisco Alvarez
6. Andrés Giménez
7. Matthew Allan
8. Brett Baty
9. Mark Vientos
10. Luis Guillorme

One glance at this list and the top-heavy nature of the Mets' young talent becomes immediately apparent. Occupying the top three positions are the reigning National League Rookie of the Year, a solid, everyday regular major league shortstop, and a player who had a breakout season in 2019 and proved he belonged at the big league level.

What more is there to write about Pete Alonso that hasn't already been written? Expectations were high for his rookie season and yet it's safe to say he exceeded them and then some. He blasted 53 home runs in 2019, the most by a rookie in baseball history. He drove in 120 runs and posted a 141 DRC+. There were concerns about his ability to connect consistently on offspeed pitches. He dispelled them quickly. There were reservations about his defense at first base. Those were cast aside as well. Not only is Alonso easily the best player on the Mets under 25 years of age, he is arguably the best player on the Mets period not named Jacob deGrom.

Amed Rosario's big league journey has been more circuitous than Alonso's, despite the more prestigious prospect pedigree at the time of his debut. In fact, the hype led many to cry "bust" before his age-24 season. But he quietly took a step forward in 2019, more than doubling his 2018 WARP total. A free swinger, Rosario's selectivity at the plate has markedly improved. While his speed and athleticism are undeniable, his highlight-reel-worthy plays in the field often belied his missteps on routine plays. But extra work with his coaching staff paid off for the young shortstop to the tune of a much better defensive performance in the second half of the season. A solid .287/.323/.432 slash line combined with continued improvements defensively made Rosario an above-average regular at shortstop in 2019.

Dominic Smith capped off his 2019 season with a moment befitting its magic—a walk-off home run to lift the Mets to victory in the bottom of the 11th in the final game of the season. This season saw Smith elevate himself from a prospect who never lived up to his potential to folk hero status. Though it's hard to imagine now, entering spring training in 2019, it was unclear whether Alonso or Smith would be the Opening Day first baseman for the Mets. Alonso hit himself into the starting lineup and never left, but Smith produced in a way that made him impossible to ignore—so much so that the Mets conducted an ill-fated experiment playing Smith in the outfield. While his defense there was horrid, his performance with the bat was not. He slashed .282/.355/.525 with a 112 DRC+ in 89 games, far eclipsing the underwhelming numbers he had posted in his short big league career prior to 2019. Unfortunately, his breakout season was cut short by a stress reaction in his left foot. His improbable walk-off home run in the season's waning hour was his first plate appearance in over two months. But with Alonso already a franchise cornerstone, Smith's future with the Mets remains uncertain, despite the massive strides he made in 2019.

Just below this tier of major leaguers is the consensus top prospect in the Mets' system, but, like many guys on this list, he is far away from the major leagues. The 5-10 spots here are virtually interchangeable and all but one of this group of players has yet to play above the Double-A level. Notably absent from this list are all of the young arms the Mets have shuttled back and forth between Triple-A and the majors over the past couple of seasons, mostly products of trades made in an attempt to bolster organizational pitching depth that never panned out. A player who has been shuttled back and forth between the big leagues and the minors a fair amount in his professional career and rounds out this list is Luis Guillorme, a glove-first middle infielder. He posted an 85 DRC+ over 70 plate appearances for the Mets in 2019, but there remains enough hope in his offensive upside to earn him an appearance here, buoyed by his elite skills in the field. The fact that all but two of the players on this list, outside of the top three established major leaguers, are not just 25 or younger, but 20 or younger, speaks volumes about the state of the Mets organization.

Part 3: Featured Articles

The Baseball Is Juiced (Again)

Robert Arthur

This article originally appeared at Baseball Prospectus on April 5, 2019.

It started when the normally reliable Chris Sale got lit up for three homers by the Mariners in the Red Sox's season opener. It was part of a record number of taters that flew on Opening Day, as starters from Sale to Zack Greinke were taken deep by the handful. Then Christian Yelich hit a home run in each of his first four games, tying yet another MLB record, this one for consecutive games with a dinger to start a season.

It didn't take long for fans and players to begin whispering and tweeting about the baseballs being juiced again. It's early yet for us to come to any definitive conclusion about the 2019 season, but preliminary data shows that the baseball has returned to its aerodynamic peak. Whether that means this season will smash home run records like 2017 did remains to be seen.

Before home run explosion over the last few years, no one worried too much about the baseball's air resistance. While MLB and Rawlings (the company that manufactures the official baseballs) kept track of dozens of metrics to make sure that the ball was consistent from month to month, they didn't measure drag.

But drag is incredibly important in determining how likely a hitter is to knock one out of the park. As baseballs become more aerodynamic, they travel further given a certain initial velocity. A deep fly ball that might have been caught at the warning track can instead go into the first row of the stands. A three percent change in drag coefficient can work to add about five feet to a well-hit fly ball, which can in turn increase home runs league wide by an astounding 10-15 percent.

It's possible to measure the aerodynamics of the baseball using the pitch-tracking radars currently in place in each MLB ballpark. By calculating the loss of speed from when the pitch is released to when it crosses the plate, you can directly measure the drag coefficient on the baseball. I first wrote about the role of decreasing drag in boosting home runs in 2017, and MLB's commission of scientists and statisticians later confirmed that the more aerodynamic baseballs in use that year were largely to blame for the spike in home runs. The same commission rejected some alternate hypotheses, like rising temperatures and a league-wide boost in launch angle pushing more balls over the fence.

The current era has featured some large fluctuations in drag coefficient, leading to first an explosion in 2016 and 2017, and then a dialing back of homers last year. Curious about the record-breaking home run tallies in the last few days, I used the same methodology to measure the aerodynamics of the baseballs so far in 2019.

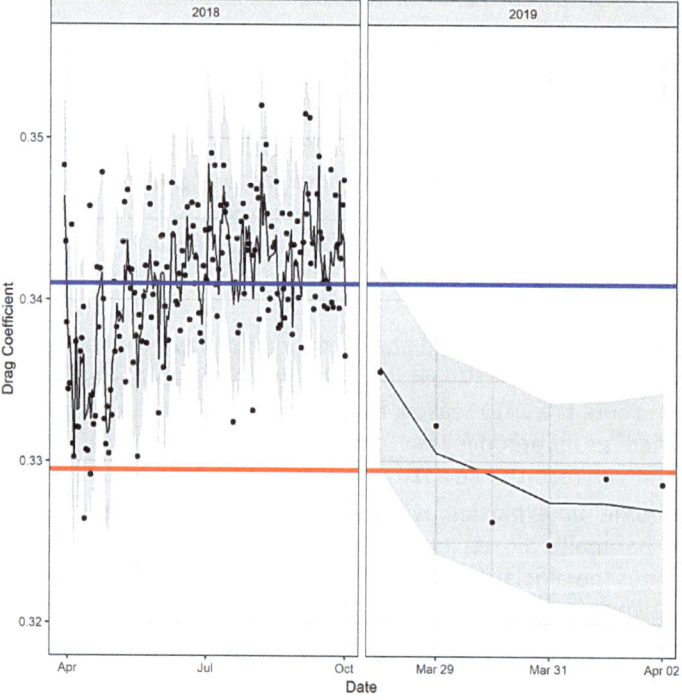

We're only a week into the 2019 season, but the drag numbers so far are among the lowest recorded in the last calendar year. With apologies for gory math, the current 2019 season average drag coefficient (the red line) would be below the 95 percent credible interval (the shaded area) for about nine-tenths of the 2018 season. (I used a Bayesian Random Walk model implemented in INLA to calculate these credible intervals, averaging the drag numbers in each game and adjusting for park.)

There were only a handful of six-day stretches in 2018 that had drag numbers below what we're seeing now, and most were in late June and early July. All of this means that 2019's data so far is quite a bit different than what we saw through most of last year.

These drag coefficients factor out the effects of temperature and air density, so they aren't a product of April cold. However, the numbers could be deceptive if the radars used to track pitches have changed from year to year. I consulted with some experts within baseball who were not aware of any specific modifications to the radar this year that could produce this pattern, but it's an important caveat of which to be aware.

On the one hand, it's only been six days, and we don't quite have the statistical basis to say that these drag coefficients are unprecedented compared to 2018. On the other hand, we've witnessed about 5,000 fastballs so far this season, so it's not as if our sample size is small. At least so far, the baseball has played like it's much more aerodynamic than it was last year. In fact, the current drag coefficient is really only comparable to 2017, when the baseballs were more aerodynamic than they had been in at least a decade.

It's not just fancy radar tracking indicating that the baseball is flying through the air more easily. The current number of home runs per game (as of this writing) is the highest it's been since the heady days of 2017, the year that teams and players broke dinger-related records everywhere you looked. That's especially remarkable considering that we're in what is typically the coldest part of the regular season, when lower temperatures and higher winds tend to suppress offense and keep balls in the air within the park. Comparing only from April to April, this year's rate of home runs per fly ball is even a little bit higher than it was in 2017.

With that said, the current measurements are no guarantee that 2019 will be another year of record-shattering homer hitting. The trouble with the drag measurements is that they are not consistent from June to August, from week to week, or even sometimes from day to day. Whether because of natural manufacturing variation or differences in the underlying supplies of cowhide and thread that go into the baseballs, drag has a tendency to fluctuate up and down over the course of a year. So the homers that fly in the first week of April wouldn't necessarily clear the fence a week later.

It's possible that this one-week drop in drag coefficient subsides and the baseball returns to its 2018 levels. On the other hand, it's almost equally probable that the ball becomes even more slippery and flies ever farther. Either way, it's clear that the baseball's air resistance is something to keep an eye on for the remainder of the 2019 season.

—*Robert Arthur is an author of Baseball Prospectus.*

The Moral Hazard of Playing It Safe

Craig Goldstein

This article originally appeared at Baseball Prospectus on August 6, 2019.

A couple days prior to the trade deadline, amidst a sea of tranquility posing as the lead up to the trade deadline, Bob Nightengale took to Twitter. Nightengale, who was probably wearing his pants backwards at the time, tweeted that MLB GMs were coming around on the idea that the unified trade deadline should be moved back from July 31 to August 15, so they could better assess their positions in the standings and whether they should buy or sell. To which I said:

This might strike some as reductive and churlish. And it might be that, but it isn't really wrong, either. Jeff Quinton wrote a great piece discussing the environmental factors that enable front offices to avoid risk without upsetting the apple cart within their own fanbases. I don't believe that it goes far enough, however. His article gives us the proper framework through which to understand why these behaviors have been allowed to seep into front offices throughout the league. Understanding the reasons behind these actions are different from excusing them, though, and GMs should not be let off the hook for their non-competitive approach to the trade deadline (much less the offseason).

⚾ ⚾ ⚾

It's fair to say that fans as a group have rarely, if ever, been pro-player. It is also fair to say that in the time during and following the Moneyball revolution, the pendulum swung from fans who cared intensely about winning in the moment (and thus might be intolerant of a rebuilding approach) to fans who supported building a team that could compete throughout multiple seasons, viewing the playoffs as a crapshoot, with the thought that getting multiple bites at the apple was a better approach than taking a bigger bite in any one season.

There's nothing wrong with that approach, and I still find merit in that argument. However, it seems that the pendulum has swung too far in that direction. Teams are overvaluing some of the individual factors that make themselves long-term contenders rather than attempting to seize a championship when given the opportunity. It's a difficult needle to thread.

And surely, they (and those in similar positions) would have liked another two weeks to clarify where they stand so as to better marshal their resources. We've all asked for a few more minutes when staring at a menu. But all of these GMs and front office personnel are where they are to make difficult decisions. They have proprietary data and internal analysts dedicated to understanding their position relative to the rest of the league, and how any move in the here and now impacts their long-term vision. To complain (if that report is accurate) that over half the season is not enough to properly assess their season is bullshit of the highest order. Move the deadline, and you'd simply have increasingly discounted trade offers because teams would be acquiring even less control of anyone they're acquiring, rental or not.

Major league front offices are behaving like the managers they lampooned two decades ago. They're effectively sacrificing a runner to second in the ninth inning—not because it's the correct move, but rather because it is safe. It used to be that the phrase "moral hazard" was used to describe general managers who made ill-fated, short-sighted decisions aimed at locking in wins and securing their jobs at the expense of their team's future. Now, general managers are guilty of committing moral hazards in the opposite direction, playing it utterly safe and terrified of becoming scapegoats.

In lieu of bold action, they opt to pussyfoot around a current window of contention, choosing instead to play the long game and stack up years of control like they're blocks in a game of Jenga. GMs pass on signing quality players in free agency because the back-end of the deal might look bad, and because they might be able to squeeze out 70 percent of the production from a player who costs a tenth as much. That's a safer investment, too, because it's also hard to prove a negative—it's impossible to prove that Manny Machado would make the Mets a playoff team in 2019-2020, but it's easy to say that the back half of Robinson Cano's contract sucks. Owners, who rule over GM's jobs, are also humans with human brain processes that will always make the so-called albatross contract uglier than the road not taken.

These days, GMs are remembered for the bad deals they make and the surplus value they generate, not the acquisition of expensive, necessary talents that meet their market worth (or fall slightly short while still providing significant on-field value). And front offices know that one or two expensive misfires can cost them their jobs, no matter how many good deals they make.

No front office exemplifies this ethos more than the Toronto Blue Jays. General Manager Ross Atkins had this to say following the Blue Jays underwhelming trade deadline:

This is by no means the first time that an executive will cite years of control to justify their actions, which is often just another way of saying "don't look at what we got, look at how much we got of it." Atkins touts quantity to elide the discussion of quality—either, that of the players acquired, or those given up. Remember: the other teams presumably value years of control, too.

Atkins also had some thoughts to offer regarding free agents back in early 2018:

New York Mets 2020

This ignores, of course, whether the player can create enough value in the front end of a contract to justify the longer term of a deal, and the decline that often occurs in the back end. It also ignores whether the player can fill a need the team requires and put them in a position to compete for and win a championship. But as teams seemingly avoid contention at all, where they might end up having to consider and later justify some of these tough decisions, we still see risk-averse approaches.

Anthony Fenech's article on two trades that recently extended GM Al Avila didn't make got at this issue rather well:

> Passing on those deals was defensible: Both players had yet to break out and trading [Michael] Fulmer—a pitcher who appeared to be a future ace, no matter his injury concerns—would have taken serious gumption, opening Avila up to strong criticism.

Avoiding strong criticism is something each of us can understand as a motivation, but the avoidance of criticism only matters if that criticism is valid. In Fulmer's case, shoving his injury concerns aside affects not only the years that the team controls him (he is currently missing a full season due to Tommy John surgery) but also the quality of those seasons, as his knee and elbow injuries combined to dampen his effectiveness even when healthy enough to pitch. But it was easy to present the then-current image of Fulmer as a top of the rotation pitcher who the team had under its domain for the next five seasons as something to build around. The status quo isn't nearly as often second-guessed as a decision that disrupts it.

⚾ ⚾ ⚾

MLB GMs are risk-averse to a fault. They are ivy-educated and consulting firm-approved, and yet they can't seem to avoid leaving wins on the table in their all-consuming lust for a non-existent $/WAR championship. They are supposed to zig when everyone else zags, and not merely pay lip service to the idea of zigging through a calculated PR plan built on convincing the fan base their approach is novel when it actually apes most of their competitors. Instead they've become far more concerned with making safe, accepted-by-the-new-common-wisdom decisions, such that our prior understanding of what a moral hazard is has become inverted.

I can't blame them entirely, and not only because of the reasons that Quinton illuminated in his article, but also because of the damage wrought by the introduction of the second wild card (WC2) spot. MLB's desire to have more teams in playoff contention has sparked anti-competitive behavior. Teams know now that they do not need to swing big as they assemble their roster because there is a good chance that a mediocre team can either catch fire and capture a division, or muddle along until they back into the WC2.

Simultaneously, the one-game playoff has neutered the WC1, putting an entire season on the flip of a coin like some sort of baseball-obsessed Anton Chigurh. While the one-game playoff makes sense as a way to increase the value of winning a division, it also means that if a front office doesn't like its chances of overcoming a behemoth like the Dodgers or Astros in the offseason, they have few incentives to chase glory. Similarly, the relative inaction in the NL Central at the trade deadline—despite a wide open division—can be explained by the idea that any high-variance investment could still result in only a wild card (or worse) result, given the mere two months left in the season to make an impact.

⚾ ⚾ ⚾

As stated at the top, we should not confuse reasons for excuses. The implementation of the second wild card is just one of many environmental factors that influence how each front office operates. I am convinced that it is one of the larger factors, but I am also convinced that organizations need to shed the yoke of "efficiency at all costs" so that they can instead pursue competition, as the spirit of the game intends. Until they do, we're all deadline losers.

—*Craig Goldstein is an author of Baseball Prospectus.*

Index of Names

Acosta, Daison 111
Adams, Matt 20
Allan, Matthew 88, 103
Alonso, Pete 22
Altherr, Aaron 94
Alvarez, Francisco 80, 102
Bashlor, Tyler 97
Baty, Brett 81, 104
Betances, Dellin 89
Brach, Brad 50
Canó, Robinson 24
Céspedes, Yoenis 82
Conforto, Michael 26
Cordell, Ryan 28
Davis, J.D. 30
Davis, Rajai 94
deGrom, Jacob 78
Díaz, Edwin 52
Dibrell, Tony 97
Espino, Sebastian 111
Familia, Jeurys 54
Flexen, Chris 56
Gagnon, Drew 97
Gilliam, Ryley 97
Gimenez, Andres 83, 103
Gómez, Carlos 32
Gonsalves, Stephen 97, 109
Gonzalez, Harol 97, 110
Gsellman, Robert 58
Guillorme, Luis 84
Haggerty, Sam 94
Hart, Donnie 97
Humphreys, Jordan 111
Kilome, Franklyn 108
Lagares, Juan 94
Lockett, Walker 97
Lowrie, Jed 85
Lugo, Seth 60
Mangum, Jake 94
Marisnick, Jake 34
Matz, Steven 62
Mauricio, Ronny 86, 101
McNeil, Jeff 36
Moroff, Max 94
Newton, Shervyen 87, 108
Nido, Tomás 38
Nimmo, Brandon 40
Nogosek, Stephen 97
Núñez, Eduardo 42
Oswalt, Corey 90
Palmer, Jaylen 109
Parker, Jarrett 94
Payano, Pedro 97
Peterson, David 91, 106
Peterson, Tim 97
Porcello, Rick 64
Pounders, Brooks 97
Ramos, Wilson 44
Rhame, Jacob 66
Rivera, Rene 94
Rosario, Amed 46
Rumbelow, Nick 97

Sanchez, Ali 94
Santana, Ervin 97
Santos, Junior 97, 107
Sewald, Paul 68
Smith, Dominic 48
Smith, Kevin 97, 109
Stroman, Marcus 70
Syndergaard, Noah 72
Szapucki, Thomas 92, 107

Valdez, Freddy 110
Ventura, Jordany 112
Vientos, Mark 94, 105
Villines, Stephen 112
Wacha, Michael 74
Wilson, Justin 76
Wolf, Josh 93, 105
Zamora, Daniel 97